The Grandparents handbook

The Grandparents handbook

JUNE LOVES

HarperCollins*Publishers*

HarperCollins_Publishers_

First published in Australia in 2000
Reprinted in 2000
by HarperCollins*Publishers* Pty Limited
ABN 36 009 913 517
A member of HarperCollins*Publishers* (Australia) Pty Limited Group
http://www.harpercollins.com.au

HarperCollins_Publishers_
25 Ryde Road, Pymble, Sydney, NSW 2073, Australia
31 View Road, Glenfield, Auckland 10, New Zealand
77–85 Fulham Palace Road, London W6 8JB, United Kingdom
Hazelton Lanes, 55 Avenue Road, Suite 2900, Toronto, Ontario M5R 3L2
and 1995 Markham Road, Scarborough, Ontario M1B 5M8, Canada
10 East 53rd Street, New York NY 10022, USA

National Library of Australia Cataloguing-in-Publication data:

Loves, June, 1938– .
    The grandparents handbook.
    ISBN 0 7322 6602 5.
    1. Grandparenting. 2. Grandparent and child.
    I. Title.
306.8745

Printed in Australia by Griffin Press Pty Ltd on 79gsm Bulky Paperback

7 6 5 4 3 2   00 01 02 03

Contents

Introduction

Grandparenting is not difficult. Just tricky. You do not need qualifications to become a grandparent. In fact you have very little to do with being a grandparent. It just happens. One day you're not a grandparent. The next day you are a grandparent.

Changes in family patterns mean that you don't need blood ties to become a grandparent or that 'special' person in a child's life. You don't even have to be that three-letter word – old – to be a grandparent. You can be an amazingly young grandparent – depending on the age of your partner. In some circumstances, through weird quirks of fate, you could become a grandparent even before you have contemplated becoming a parent!

Happily most grandparents are naturally endowed with the necessary qualities needed for grandparenting – common sense and experience.

All but the heartless would agree that being a grandparent brings the greatest joy. Absolute delirious happiness. There is nothing in the whole world like a small person placing their hand in yours in complete trust. A squashy bear-hug and a sloppy kiss from an adored small person is bliss.

To hold that special little person in your arms is the ultimate in love, contentment and fulfilment.

However . . . however . . . not every grandparenting experience is a garden of roses. Sometimes . . . sometimes . . . when you return home from a visit to the grandchildren, or when you close the door as the last little grandchild disappears down the garden path, you can be left an absolute wreck. A former shadow of your vital, energetic, enthusiastic, independent self.

This book will help you to survive grandparenting intact. It is full of useful, practical tips and information to enable you to be an adoring, doting grandparent of the highest order – yet still maintain your sanity and health.

Part One:
You don't need a degree but . . .

Battening down the hatches

It is wise to batten down the hatches before your grandchildren visit your home. You, your grandchildren, your pets and your belongings all need care so they can be preserved!

Take basic, sensible precautions in preparation for visits by your little darlings to ensure safety and peace of mind for everyone and avoid guilt and embarrassment.

Secure and safe

Your grandchildren have the right to be safe and secure in your home and environment.

Safety precautions around your home, outdoors and when visiting your grandchildren do not have to be doom or gloom procedures. But safety first is an absolute necessity and top priority.

Changes will be needed to maintain a safe environment. You can make changes for each visit or permanent changes. Once this is done endless hours of enjoyment stretch before you in the company of your grandchildren.

As grandchildren grow older you can reassess your home and garden. However, you will probably find new grandchildren keep arriving on the scene and you will need constant vigilance for their safety and yours.

Remember, nine out of ten accidents can be predicted and prevented.

Checklist

- ☑ Lock Scruffy and Fluff in laundry.
- ☑ Remove precious vases and ornaments from coffee tables or push them back on shelves.
- ☑ Lock study.
- ☑ Lock shed.
- ☑ Clear and check the garden.
- ☑ Take medicine from bedside tables and place out of grandchildren's reach.
- ☑ Stock up on food and drink.

Check at child level

Get down on your hands and knees. At small child level, check the risks in your home and garden.

What could be a hazard?

How can you make a safer environment for your grandchildren when they visit?

Take a pad and pencil as you move from room to room.

List potential hazards so you can safeguard your home and environment.

Safety first around the house

A little care and thought can prevent accidents and make sure your grandchildren are safe and happy in your home.

Fire safety

The main causes of home fires are electrical faults and unattended cooking equipment.

Most fires occur in the kitchen, bedrooms and lounge rooms.

These facts are important to remember because it is easy to be distracted with young children in your home.

Safety tips for peace of mind

☛ Install safety switches which cut power off within a thirteenth of a heartbeat.

☛ Use power point covers to stop children poking anything into them.

☛ Run cold water into the bath first. Never leave children unattended.

☛ Run cold water for a shower first and then add hot water.

☛ Do not use portable floor-level heaters in bathrooms.

☛ Use cordless jugs and irons to reduce the chance of children pulling appliances on to themselves.

☛ Ensure medicines and household cleaners are out of reach of children.

☛ Never have a hot drink when holding a child.

Fire safety tips

☛ Install and maintain smoke alarms and fire extinguishers.

☛ Buy a fire rug.

☛ Plan and practise fire drill with a home escape, for example, 'If there's a fire we'll hurry to the front gate!' Be lighthearted but firm.

☛ Keep matches and flammable liquids in a safe place.

☛ Make sure children respond to the commands, DON'T TOUCH! HOT!'

Checklist to avoid burns and scalds

☑ Have you checked your water thermostat? You will not have a worry if you turn it down to 48.9 degrees, which is a safe temperature.

☑ Are all pot handles turned away from the stove front?

☑ Are there any appliance cords dangling within a child's reach?

☑ Can you keep the children away from the stove or microwave when you are cooking?

Poisons

All children are at risk from poisons kept around the house. Children from one to three are most at risk. Keep all medicines, poisons and cleaning products locked away – out of grandchildren's sight and reach.

Know what poisons you have. Many things found around the house, such as cleaning products, sedatives and tranquillisers, liquid drugs and ointments are dangerous to children. If you are not sure whether they're poisonous, check the labels.

Safety hints . . .

- ☛ Install child-resistant latches on cupboard where you store poisonous products.
- ☛ Store poisonous substances in a childproof container and in a safe place.
- ☛ Keep cleaners in a safe place.
- ☛ Look for cleaning products packaged in resealable, child proof containers.
- ☛ Keep cleaning products in their original containers; do not, for example, transfer them to a juice bottle.
- ☛ When in use, close the container immediately and place up high as a temporary safeguard.
- ☛ Buy enough oven cleaner for one use only. Avoid keeping it in the house.
- ☛ Throw out any medicines you are not using.
- ☛ Put a lock on your medicine cupboard.
- ☛ Don't keep any medication on bedside tables or in drawers.
- ☛ Never refer to medication as a 'sweet'. (Headache pills, and vitamins in large quantities, can be very dangerous to children.)

Safety outdoors

You will need to take steps to make a safe outdoor environment and a secure playing place for your grandchildren.

☞ Clear away junk and things children might trip over. Check for sharp edges which could hurt them.
☞ Cut off sharp branches that hang at child's eye level.
☞ Have regular household clean-ups to remove junk.
☞ Clean out garages and sheds. Or keep them securely locked.
☞ Make sure fences are strong, with no protruding nails or splinters. Secure loose boards where little grandchildren could squeeze through and escape your care.
☞ Make sure you have childproof locks on any gate with access to the road or lanes.

Playground equipment

If you have playground equipment, such as a swing or slide, check it regularly. Make sure it is stable with no sharp edges and is situated away from garden paths. Supervise play on swings so that a small child cannot be hit by another using the swing. Rubber swings are best.

Chip bark or similar material should be under play equipment to cushion falls. Trampolines can be dangerous. A trampoline should be set in the ground. Only one child at a time should use it.

Dog safety in and outdoors

☞ Any type of pet dog can be a risk to grandchildren. Some dogs are fiercely territorial. Keep an eye on the grandchildren when they are around your pets. Even a friendly dog may bite.
☞ If you are unsure of your dog's behaviour around children, it is best to put the dog in a secure separate area or tie it up.

Water safety

Children love water in any form. It is an enormous attraction! Think . . . does a little child ever walk around a puddle? No! Never! Young children have no fear of water whatsoever . . . or the ability to save themselves.

Always carefully watch children near water. Pools, spas, ponds, baths – even nappy buckets are hidden danger areas. Remember children can drown in as little as five centimetres of water. Always supervise small children in the bath.

Do not allow children to play in the laundry or bathroom unattended.

Water safety checklist

☑ Cover ornamental fish ponds with wire.

☑ Empty paddling pools after use.

☑ Always empty baths after use.

Pool and spa safety

A safety fence separating the house from the pool is the most important safeguard. It should always be maintained with a self-closing, self-latching gate. There should be nothing nearby that children could use to climb over it. In many states and countries this is mandatory.

Outdoor spas should be fenced in the same way as swimming pools. All spas should have a fixed cover.

Indoor spas should have a lockable door. Empty them straight after use.

Sun safety

You can teach your grandchildren to protect themselves from the sun at an early age, regardless of their skin type and colouring. Once a tan was a sign of health. Today we realise it is a sign of ultraviolet radiation damage. You cannot 'toughen up' children's skin or protect them by building up a tan.

Precautions to take

☛ Encourage children to play in the shade wherever possible – especially between 11 am and 3 pm daylight saving time and between 10 am and 2 pm non-daylight saving time.

☛ Make sure grandchildren wear a legionnaire-style hat, a broadbrimmed hat or a sun visor with side flaps. They give extra protection for the ears and necks.

☛ Grandchildren should wear loose-fitting T-shirts, preferably with long sleeves, a high neck and collar. Alternatively there is 'neck-to-knee' swimwear especially designed to resist harmful rays.

☛ Apply a broad spectrum, water-resistant SPF30+ sunscreen regularly. Apply frequently when grandchildren are in and out of the water.

☛ Remember UV rays penetrate at least twenty centimetres in the water. Apply a zinc cream or lip screen to sensitive areas such as lips, nose and ears.

☛ Babies under twelve months should not be deliberately exposed to the sun at all.

On the farm

Grandparents who live on farms are a fortunate and popular breed. Keeping children happy is never a worry when grandchildren visit a farm.

Such lucky grandparents rarely need a 'Things to do indoors' list. Grandchildren are usually so exhausted from activity and fresh air that they sleep like logs.

Farms are an exciting and challenging environment for children. Whether you are holidaying there with your grandchildren, or you live on a farm, there can be some hazards that need to be checked.

These will vary from property to property.

Farm safety tips

☛ Provide a safe area for playing near your house – preferably fenced off from farming activities, dams and livestock.

☛ Clean up old junk and remove old machinery and woodpiles from where children play.

☛ Keep young grandchildren away from tractors and farm machinery.

☛ Supervise older grandchildren around tractors and farm machinery when they help with farm work.

☛ Make silos inaccessible by removing the lower steps.

☛ Insist that helmets are worn for horse- and bike-riding.

☛ Before moving machinery check that no children are about.

☛ Store tools, chemicals and all equipment, including old machinery, well away from where children play.

At the beach

Many grandparents live at the beach. If you do, families will love to visit and have holidays with you. The beach can be a fascinating place for young grandchildren to discover all the wonders of the sea and shore. However, grandchildren and families need to be aware of the dangers and take some safety precautions.

Surf beaches are particularly dangerous for children. If your grandchildren haven't been in the surf before, arrange for them to have some instruction from lifesavers about how and where to swim. Some lifesaving clubs run programs for children during the summer holidays.

Beach safety tips

☛ Swim only at beaches patrolled by lifesavers.
☛ Make sure grandchildren swim between the safety flags in full view of a lifesaver.
☛ Be vigilant when you are looking after small children. They tend to all look the same in bathers, and can move a long way from you in their play.
☛ Don't swim after a meal.

Handy beach hints

☛ Keep a supply of hats and sunscreen at your home.
☛ Beach umbrellas or shelters will also make life easier.
☛ Take a supply of cool drinks and play equipment to the beach as well as a comfortable beach chair for yourself.
☛ Visit the beach early in the morning or late in the afternoon when you can avoid the sun at its strongest.
☛ Set up an outdoor shower to sluice off unwanted sand from little bodies before they come into the house.
☛ Grandchildren can have their own towels and an easy-access area where they can hang up their rinsed swimmers and towels after a swim.

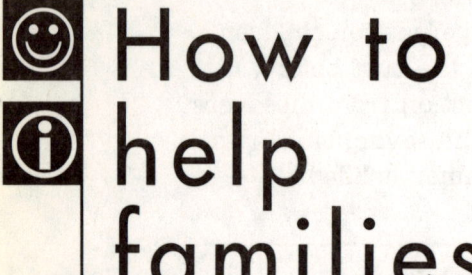

How to help families

Sympathetic listening

Sympathetic listening is a great support for families, and grandparents can be experts. Make sure you are always available to listen in a warm, friendly manner. Often, when a worried parent discusses problems with a sympathetic grandparent, solutions and outcomes become obvious. But don't rush in with remedies and good advice. Your 'good advice' could be devastating to a parent's self-esteem. The last thing a worried parent needs is some 'expert' telling them what to do.

Regular visits to your place

Although the traditional Sunday afternoon visits to grandparents is a fast-fading custom, regular visits to your place can become, in modern terms, 'quality time relief' – relaxation for everyone concerned.

Watch that regular visits don't turn into horror outings for the family and yourself. A little planning will help enormously.

☛ Provide a simple meal. Don't make a fuss. Explain to parents that you are quite happy for them to leave whenever they feel like it.

☛ It may help busy working parents if you arrange to pick up grandchildren from school on the night of the family visit. You could help with homework (see pages 82–88).

☛ Provide a simple meal for young grandchildren before adults' dining time. Young grandchildren can be bathed and in pyjamas (if you have spare ones at your place) for a smooth transition to bedtime when their parents arrive home.

☛ Make the visit a pleasant time together, a welcome event which gives children an opportunity to play and where adults can talk and children can join in.

Babysitting

Combining parenting and earning a living is an exhausting job for many parents. So offering to babysit can be life-saving for them. However, don't go overboard with too many generous offers. Watch your energy levels.

☛ Offer to babysit and make sure parents actually go out and relax while you do.

☛ Don't be afraid to say 'no' occasionally if it doesn't suit you, and you won't be so easily taken for granted.

Financial help

You may have some excess funds by the time you become a grandparent. Helping with special projects such as buying baby equipment or paying for music lessons for a talented grandchild can be a joy for you and a great help to parents.

On the other hand make sure you don't over-commit yourself. It is important to be even-handed to avoid resentment among siblings and their partners.

Be careful you don't sign official documents without fully understanding what you are signing.

Use the advice of one or more financial advisers if you are worried about arrangements.

Remember grandparents still have a lot of living to do and need ample funds.

Grandparents Golden Rule

Never preach, teach, judge or compare!

Grieving

The death of a baby or a child creates immeasurable sadness in a family. Many parents and grandparents would have already begun to visualise the joy of the baby growing, or of playing with a toddler in the park, and of planning the child's future. They grieve not only for the baby they have lost but for the future they had planned for the child, and their part in it.

Parents and grandparents need to have the opportunity to express their feelings of grief. There are organisations that support bereaved parents, where they can meet other bereaved parents and feel less isolated.

The need to mourn the death of a baby is often underestimated in our society. Memorial services, or other forms of public remembrance, are important in recognising the loss of a child and can give a sense of peace and resolution.

Supporting the family

☞ Grandparents, while grieving themselves, can help families in many practical ways during this sad time. Keeping a household running or providing babysitting for other children can give parents space and time in which to start picking up their everyday lives again.

Celebrations

Grandparents are celebration experts! They have conquered the art of taking something ordinary and turning it into something extraordinary.

The ritual of tea-time – real tea in a teapot, milk in a jug, sugar in a bowl, a tea-strainer, the best cups and saucers, a few sandwiches and a cake – can become a special ceremony to be shared with grandchildren, the family and friends.

Wise grandparents know the importance of ceremonies and celebrations for grandchildren. They create fond, childhood memories to be recalled with pleasure.

Survival tactics for family celebrations

Sometimes – only sometimes thank goodness – a family celebration can seem like a battleground with all the odds stacked against you.

When the family togetherness wanes or the going gets tough . . . escape. Plead a headache – tiredness – whatever. Find a hiding place or leave. There will be plenty of time later when you can play the role of peace-maker and negotiator.

Another alternative is to grab some company – family or grandchildren – and go for a walk. There is nothing like a brisk walk to restore one's equilibrium.

Avoiding trouble

If families really don't get along it is best to stay away from each other. Christmas and other special times of celebration can be a time of great stress for families for many reasons.

If you sense that the thought of Christmas or some other occasion looms as a time of stress for your family, gain help from counselling services.

Inviting an outsider to your celebration will often provide the incentive for everyone to be on their best behaviour.

If you cannot see any hope of a pleasant time – don't go! Return visits where you will only be involved with one set of relatives at a time and you are ensured of a peaceful visit.

Being a go-between

When children are involved in a dispute between parents, grandparents may successfully act as go-betweens.
For example, grandchildren can spend Christmas Eve with their mother and her extended family. On Christmas morning grandparents can meet them somewhere in between. They can then take them on to have Christmas lunch with their father and his parents.

Parties

Family parties are
easy to organise, and
grandparents are
excellent organisers
and communicators.
Parties don't
necessarily require
large amounts of
money . . . just time.

Grandparent party helpers

If you are a helper let the family know exactly what you will contribute such as 'the' cake or other food. Let the family know if you will be available for catering jobs such as setting the table, decorating the room or the last minute arranging and serving of food. Knowing your exact job description avoids complications!

Checklist

You will need to arrange:
- ☑ the time;
- ☑ the place – indoor and outdoor venue – in case of adverse weather;
- ☑ the guest list;
- ☑ the food – the simpler the better;
- ☑ a cake – if there is going to be a cake cutting ceremony;
- ☑ music and entertainment . . . 'not the compulsory kind!'
- ☑ helpers of all ages.

Childrens parties

Arranging a party for grandchildren can often become the domain of grandparents. A party for grandchildren doesn't have to be a celebration that breaks the budget. A very successful party – one where all the young guests have a great time – can be arranged on the most modest of budgets.

Good entertainment and lots of inexpensive food are the key to success. Enlist friends and every relative you can find to help you make an inexpensive and fun party.

Consider:

☛ When to hold the party and for how long. Include a starting and finishing time, where the party is to be held and a contact number (two hours is about the limit for young children).

☛ Where . . . at your home or another venue like the zoo. If you are holding the party outdoors have an alternative indoor venue in case of bad weather. What you're looking for is a place with space!

☛ Bite-sized pieces of whatever are your traditional dishes, little sandwiches with healthy fillings and fresh fruit salad will be received with enthusiasm by children.

☛ Traditional favourites like homemade sausage rolls, cocktail sausages, jelly and chocolate frogs, are also good standbys. And of course fruit juice and lemonade to drink.

The cake

A cake with candles is a priority for the candle blowing rituals.

It needs to be big enough so each child can go home with a piece of cake wrapped in a paper napkin.

Party games

Party games should be fun. Don't pressure little guests. Have inexpensive gifts for prizes. Make sure that everyone eventually goes home with a prize. (Turn to Games to Play, page 213 for ideas.)

Theme parties

Theme parties are fun for young grandchildren. How about a ghost party, teddy bears' picnic, pirates' party . . . the list is endless. Have the table and room decorated accordingly. Extend the theme to food where possible.

Party entertainers!

Some grandparents make fantastic party entertainers. Can you draw lightning sketches of guests, perform magic, tell great stories? How would you feel dressed up as a fairy, a clown, or a wizard?

If this idea appeals to you, go for it. Polish up your act! You could be a raging success. You could even go into your own party entertaining business!

The Role of the Birthday Grandchild

Gently encourage the birthday child to thank guests personally for their gifts.

Let's party somewhere else!

If you would like the party action to take place somewhere other than your living room, there are lots of other options, such as the park, where you can bring your own party picnic or barbecue. Look for a safe play area and a sheltered place to eat!

Better still, there are lovely people – 'party experts' – who, as long as you can pay the bill, will provide the perfect party with food and supervised entertainment. An idea worth thinking about!

Teenage parties . . .

'Can I have my sixteenth party at your house, Gran?'

If you are asked to be the party provider do not jump in immediately! Take time to think about it!

Today teenage parties are an enormous responsibility for parents and that will include you, the grandparents, if you are giving the party.

Teenage celebrations can provide problems. You must be sure you can control a teenage party if you are asked to be the party provider. Parents, and grandparents, owe it to other parents to ensure a party doesn't get out of hand.

First check with your grandchild's family. Why aren't they being asked to give the party? If you agree to give a party for your teenager, first set out rules and guidelines. You must be able to enlist the support of your family and you will also need other parents or adults on hand to help.

Guidelines for a teenage party

☞ A guest list with limited numbers, who are sent invitations.

☞ Established start and finish times – a reasonable end for a sixteen's party is 12 o'clock. If any guest is going to leave early tell them you will be phoning parents to let them know. Guests are to picked up by a known person.

☞ A guest who is an unknown partner of a friend will be checked with the family. They should be introduced before the party.

☞ The party to be in one party area – one space (could be in a hired venue).

☞ Gates or doors in your home to be closed. Bags to be stored in a safe place.

☞ Gate crashers – unwanted party goers – to be asked to leave as soon as they arrive.

☞ You will be holding an alcohol-free party for your grandchild. For support, check details, especially check with the legal authorities in your state.

Grandparents Golden Rule

Your teenage grandchild may not like your rules and may drop their party plans. Do not worry. You have a right to protect your grandchild and prospective guests, and your home.

On the other hand, your teenage grandchild may appreciate the fairness of these limits and will feel cared for by you and their parents.

Money management

Some grandparents
have a surplus of
money – others need
to manage their
finances with care.

Budgeting

When you are involved and having fun with your grandchildren, money can disappear very quickly.

Costs of recreational entertainment can quickly add up to an alarming amount: films, amusement parks and eating out, etc., without counting the-spur-of-moment purchases such as a desired pair of jeans, book or toy. If you are indulgent grandparents, you could be paying off credit cards and accounts long after your grandchildren have gone home.

To avoid going over your budget, estimate the cost before promising treats.

Share budget planning

Plan a budget with your grandchildren. This is an effective way to keep within your means. Inquiring and estimating entrance costs, family tickets, fares and parking for a planned activity will help keep your budget under control.

Sprinkling 'materialistic' days (days that involve activities that have a cost) among 'non-materialistic' days – that is being outdoors – is a great way to have fun and keep within your budget.

Pocket money

Pocket money can be an issue when grandchildren are on a short- or long-term stay with you, if you are providing it. Allocating pocket money for their stay can help your budget and give them some independence in what they spend and how they spend it.

Grandparents have to decide whether to give pocket money or not. If the family agrees, then you need to work out whether chores are required for the money.

Most grandparents agree that sharing jobs is the way to go. It's fantastic if grandchildren can gain pleasure from contributing and sharing responsibility within the home without monetary gain.

Some grandparents are happy to just give grandchildren spending money for outings. The children can then choose what they will spend their money on throughout the day. This can prevent constant requests for items like ice creams.

Learning the value of money

Some grandparents like the idea of grandchildren learning the value of money: how to spend and how to save! You can choose to pay grandchildren for household chores while they stay with you. Young grandchildren can earn pocket money for making beds, setting the table, etc. Consider:

☞ Are some household chores worth more than others? What will be your rates of pay? Hourly or a set rate per job.

☞ Are you going to pay the same rate to each grandchild no matter what their age, that is will the seven-year-old grandchild have opportunities to earn the same as your fifteen-year-old grandchild?

☞ If you have older grandchildren, would you organise for them to do outside jobs for friends, cleaning windows, gardening, to earn pocket money?

Time management

Time is a commodity in today's society, and there are ever-increasing demands on what seems to be an ever-decreasing supply. Thankfully time is something that most grandparents have in abundance, something they don't have to ration.

Grandparent Golden Goals

1 Keep your grandchildren happy.

2 Keep a little personal time and space for yourself so you won't be too exhausted to keep your grandchildren happy.

'Time management' is a common term in today's world. The 'experts' advise us: if we use time more efficiently we will get greater productivity.

Grandparenting does not involve working with products, thank goodness. However, a little time management when grandparenting doesn't go amiss. Planning and prioritising helps to make the most of the time we have with our grandchildren.

Basic time management techniques

☞ Keep simple action charts. List activities for the day in half-hour blocks, for example details of meals, visits to the library or park, and so on.

☞ Be flexible. It is every grandparent's right to abandon time management techniques and plans, and act with the utmost spontaneity.

Cups of coffee and friendly, neighbourly chats when grandchildren are visiting can be a problem. Young children seem able to discover endless opportunities to involve themselves in trouble when they see you are distracted with friends and neighbours.

Plan ahead. Let your friends know of your grandchildren's visits. Arrange visits with friends after your grandchildren have left for home.

Resting time

Adequate rest involves a 'Time management' strategy for grandparents when they're looking after young grandchildren for long or even short periods of time. You have to manage time so you get your usual rest and sleep. Grandparents have excellent memories. They can remember the sleepless nights that are part of the parenting package – the desperate scrambling in the dark trying to comfort their young children.

Sleep deprivation is not so bad in the short-term, but sleep becomes critical when looking after grandchildren for a long time.

Self-preservation schedule

☛ Be prepared to drop everything – the dishes can wait – and grab a nap whenever the grandchildren sleep.

☛ Some grandchildren crash when the sun goes down. Others are night owls! They never want to sleep – ever! You are in big trouble when there is a combination of sleeping patterns. This is the time to use the 'Grandparent's Basic Sleep Rule'.

☛ Opt for short-term care of grandchildren if there is a reasonable choice! Remember you are not as young as you used to be.

Sleeping

When grandchildren
are staying with you,
or you're looking after
them in their home,
getting them into bed
can be tricky.

Bedtime strategies

Keep to your grandchild's bedtime routine as much as possible, for example, dinner, a play, bath and a bedtime story. This will make it easier for them to settle.

Give grandchildren plenty of warning and preparation, for instance tell them, 'Only ten minutes to play before it is bedtime!' or 'As soon as this TV program finishes it is bedtime!'

Stick to your time limits!

Discourage starting a new game or watching a new TV program just before bedtime.

Take your phone off the hook or use your message machine when you're putting grandchildren to bed. Interruptions can set you back to square one!

Say 'Good night' and leave the room quietly and quickly.

If your grandchild comes out of the bedroom take them back gently and firmly, but immediately.

The Grandparent Golden Rule

'We all go to sleep when Grandpa or Grandma says, 'It's time to go to sleep!'

Some sleeping hints

☞ A bedside lamp or night light and soft music, as well as their favourite cuddly toy, can help settle a grandchild.

☞ Avoid using bedtime as a punishment.

☞ Don't tell bedtime stories that are too scary.

☞ To stop grandchildren from falling out of bed, place the bed against the wall. Put cushions or some other 'landing pad' on the floor next to the bed to soften a possible fall.

☞ Tuck the top sheet lengthwise so there is a good tuck-in on each side to hold the grandchild firmly in bed.

or

☞ Let them sleep on a mattress on the floor. But remember your back!

Daytime routine

If you are able to keep to the family routine, with a bit of luck your grandchild will take a daytime nap when you are caring for them.

However, see that you don't allow excessive daytime sleep. Put naps back earlier in the day to make sure your grandchild is sleepy around bedtime.

Playing soothing music just loud enough for them to hear can encourage a reluctant sleeper. Otherwise try negotiating a time set aside for rest and quiet.

Early wakers

If your grandchild is old enough to understand, you can have a clock in their room, and show them where the hands need to be before they can get up. A toy clock with the hands set at the correct time will allow them to easily tell when the right time arrives.

Depending on the age of grandchildren, you can encourage early wakers to amuse themselves quietly in the morning while you try to get a little more sleep.

☞ Try leaving some safe toys and books where they can reach them.

☞ A safe activity such as puzzles or crayons and paper on a table near their bed will be a surprise when they wake the next morning.

☞ If grandchildren keep getting out of bed for a drink, leave a drink bottle fitted with its own straw beside the bed.

Night lights and lamps

To check on your grandchildren while they are asleep, and/or to find your own way around when you are staying in the family's home, use soft emergency lights that plug into normal outlets. One or two of these lights should be part of every grandparent's survival kit: one for your room, and one for the hall – a wonderful investment.

What's for dinner?

Thinking of food to serve grandchildren and their families can be stressful.

Check so you know what grandchildren will, or might, eat! Some grandchildren have very peculiar likes and dislikes – and these can change from day to day!

Remember, there is no way that you can change a grandchild's eating pattern or behaviour during the time they spend with you. The aim is to keep grandchildren and their families happy and at the same time serve healthy meals.

Dining in

- ☛ Prepare the dining area in your home. Put down sheets of plastic or protective material under, and around, the high chair to your table for baby or toddler grandchildren. If you have a precious table with a beautiful surface, protect that too.
- ☛ Set the table with cutlery that young children can handle easily.
- ☛ Use small cups with big handles, or lids, and unbreakable plates and bowls.
- ☛ Use washable table-cloths or mats.

Picnics

Picnics are great fun! Why not picnic in your garden or the local park? This is a great alternative to eating at home and saves enormous wear and tear on your dining room!

Check on grandchildren's and the family's favourite foods.

Make finger-sized sandwiches, and pies and cakes that everyone will like. Pack fruit and juice. Bottles of frozen water will keep food cool.

Take a waterproof picnic rug or lightweight tables and chairs.

Relax! Enjoy the company of your grandchildren and family in the fresh air!

Have a garbage-free picnic.

This means using napkins and containers for food, cutlery and crockery that can be taken home, washed and re-used. An interesting challenge for all in today's disposable society.

Barbecues

Barbecues are another great eating idea to use when grandchildren and families visit. Cooking on a barbecue can fill up large spaces of time as well as providing healthy and delicious food.

If you don't have a barbecue at home, check out your nearest public barbecue in a park or garden nearby. Include grandchildren in the preparation right from the start, or have food and equipment ready to pick up and go when the grandchildren and family arrive.

Barbecue safety hints

- ☛ Supervise young grandchildren around a barbecue.
- ☛ Check that your barbecue is stable. Store a portable barbecue away when not in use.
- ☛ Take care with lighting fluids, hot plates and spitting oils and fats when cooking.

Dining out with grandchildren

Dining out with your grandchildren is not an impossibility. Some restaurant staff think it is perfectly normal to have children in their restaurant.

Other restaurants do not want to know you, sometimes with due cause. Some energetic, but adorable grandchildren do not cope well with sitting still for long in a crowded, noisy place.

Babies

Miraculously, some babies sleep throughout their restaurant visits; others will scream the whole time. If your grandchildren come under the second heading, give restaurants a miss until they are older. Instead babysit and give the parents the opportunity to not only dine out but have an uninterrupted conversation over dinner as well.

Toddlers and pre-schoolers

Babies grow into toddlers and pre-schoolers. Some toddler and pre-school grandchildren take to restaurants like ducks to water; others turn a restaurant or cafe into a battlefield. If this is the case, wait until your grandchildren grow older. Offer babysitting as an alternative.

Dining out checklist

☑ Is it a friendly, lively, informal restaurant or cafe?

☑ Are they happy to have a baby or young children as customers? (The restaurant will need extra space for a pram or capsule. As well they will not want to seat you near a couple having a romantic night out.)

☑ Are there non-smoking areas?

☑ Are there easily accessible toilets?

☑ Do they have high chairs or booster seats?

☑ Does their menu cater for children, for instance can you get a bowl of chips and a glass of apple juice?

☑ What are their opening times? Book and be early! This way you can have eaten and left before the grandchildren become tired or grumpy.

Older grandchildren

There is no reason why you can't introduce older grandchildren to the pleasure of eating out. Dress up and make it a special treat.

It's good for them to know how to behave in a restaurant – to enjoy but not be intimidated by the ritual of being served and eating good food.

Hints for a peaceful meal

Be prepared to play and talk with your grandchildren.

Take small favourite toys, one or two books, a notepad and small packet of coloured pencils so grandchildren can be entertained quietly!

Take disposable wipes for messy eaters or the occasional accident. If it all gets too hard, call for the bill and pack up. Retreat with dignity! Try eating out another time.

Balanced family meals

Good nutrition is about eating a wide variety of foods. Food can be divided into three food groups: **Eat Most, Eat Moderately** and **Eat Least.**

The **Eat Most** group includes foods such as grains and breads, fruit and vegetables.

The **Eat Moderately** group includes foods such as meat, poultry, fish, eggs, and dairy products.

The **Eat Least** group includes fats and sugars.

Modify family recipes

Don't throw away favourite family recipes. Modify them by, for example, reducing the amount of sugar used in cakes and biscuits. Add dried fruits for that extra sweet taste and more fibre.

Use as little butter, margarine and oil as possible, or leave it out.

Invest in a non-stick frypan which enables you to use minimum or no fat.

Offer snacks to grandchildren from the **Eat Most** food group such as crumpets, fruit, popcorn and raisin bread.

Offer milk and water instead of highly sweetened drinks such as cordial.

Feeding toddlers

Feeding your toddler grandchildren can be tricky, especially if they are fussy eaters. The thing to remember is that this is not your long-term job. Your grandchildren will survive until their parents take control again.

Dos and don'ts of toddler feeding

☛ **Do** protect yourself and the eating area – use bibs, aprons, plastic sheeting.

☛ **Do** have damp wipes and a mop and bucket handy.

☛ **Do** make sure you know exactly what the grandchild will eat and how to prepare it – mushed or slightly lumpy – how long it needs to be heated and how much is likely to be eaten.

☛ **Don't** have the television on or leave toys around to distract your grandchild from eating.

☛ **Don't** make the mealtime a battleground. Never force-feed a child.

☛ **Don't** provide alternative food – it may not be suitable.

☛ **Don't** panic. Their parents will be home soon.

Reluctant eaters

This will not be a problem when your grandchildren are at your house . . . just remove the meal when they have had enough. They will be hungry by next mealtime.

Don't worry about reluctant eaters when you are at their place, although you could suggest to a desperate parent – at the right time, in a friendly non-threatening way – to remove the meal when small reluctant eaters say they have had enough.

A healthy menu for older grandchildren

It's not difficult to provide variations on healthy food for older grandchildren.

Small serves are a good idea. This prevents grandparents and their pets becoming overweight from eating leftovers – and grandchildren can always return for seconds.

- ☛ **Breakfast**: Cereal and milk, fruit and toast.
- ☛ **Mid-morning snack**: Fruit or plain biscuits and cheese, a sandwich.
- ☛ **Lunch**: Soup and bread, fruit, drink of milk or yoghurt, or a sandwich filled with cheese, spreads or salad fillings.
- ☛ **Afternoon or after-school snack**: Milk drink, toast or plain biscuits.
- ☛ **Dinner**: A balanced family meal (from the **Eat Most** and **Eat Moderately** food groups).

Emergency rations

Keeping a supply of emergency rations on hand can solve potential catering problems which arrive with unexpected visits from grandchildren and families.

An emergency rations list

☞ Canned fruits, especially apricots, plums and peaches (Use for desserts or at breakfast)

☞ A range of pastas and rices

☞ Frozen icecream and yoghurt

☞ Tomato sauces – to go with pastas

☞ Supply of long-term milk – UHT, powdered, canned etc.

☞ Frozen peas and other vegetables

☞ Fresh onions and potatoes

☞ Cheese

☞ Ingredients or prepared mixes to make cakes, pancakes and scones

☞ Variety of spreads, for example peanut butter, jams, jellies and preserves

☞ Canned fish – for example tuna, salmon

☞ Basic breakfast cereals

☞ Tea and coffee (for you)

☞ Cocoa or chocolate drink mix.

What to cook

- Pizzas – make your own bases or decorate a base already made
- Shortbread biscuits – use amusing cutters (young children can decorate biscuits as insects, faces, etc.)
- Cakes that can be used in lunch boxes, chocolate and other cakes to impress adults
- Pikelets, pancakes, etc.
- Scones and simple bread recipes
- Egg dishes, for example omelettes, French toast for a breakfast menu
- Fruit salad
- Pasta dishes
- Simple main dishes that require baking, grilling or frying such as baked potatoes, grilled cheese on toast, fried chicken
- Desserts such as baked rice pudding, bread and butter puddings, apple crumble, fruit salad and baked apples.

Sandwiches

Sandwiches are healthy and great food to feed grandchildren.

Sandwiches have been a hit since the late 18th century. This was when the fourth Earl of Sandwich ordered his chef to prepare something he could eat easily at the gaming table.

Today there is an enormous variety of bread and fillings to choose from. Young grandchildren will delight in preparing their own sandwiches. They can use fancy biscuit cutters to cut them into different shapes.

Older grandchildren can invent their own gourmet sandwiches.

Grandchildren in the kitchen

Cooking is fun! Cooking can give grandchildren confidence and independence as well as – hopefully – a delicious reward at the end.

Young grandchildren can work with you as assistants. Older grandchildren can be taught how to cook a simple meal and use a microwave oven, toaster and kitchen equipment safely.

Don't despair if a teenage grandchild can't cook! In one or two sessions a grandparent can teach them to survive well in the kitchen.

Assistant chefs

- Very young grandchildren can help by doing small jobs such as cutting bananas for fruit salad, grating cheese or decorating cakes.
- Six- to eight-year-olds will need you to light the oven for them.
- Stove-top cooking can be undertaken by grandchildren of about eight years plus – with constant supervision and/or help with lighting the stove top!
- Be on hand to assist ten years plus grandchildren. Let them ask for help. Explain that even the greatest chefs in the world have assistants.

Safety in the Kitchen

Almost all cooking involves heat and heat is dangerous. Grandparents should be on hand either to light, or supervise the lighting of the oven or stove tops. Gas guns are safer than matches!

Oven cloths or pot holders should be used for hot containers and pots. Judge the weight of pots and dishes to ensure children can lift them easily and safely.

Use knives and other kitchen equipment correctly yourself, and supervise the children closely while they use them.

Teaching grandchildren to cook

Teach grandchildren to cook things they will enjoy eating, and that you and their parents will also enjoy.

- Begin with grandchildren's favourite flavours and smells – food they love to eat.
- Suggest a menu, but let grandchildren make the final decisions.
- Take grandchildren shopping for ingredients. Use food from your garden when possible.
- Explain kitchen safety rules, for instance, 'When using a knife cut away from you.'
- Always wash everyone's hands before starting to cook.
- Wear an apron. Tie hair back.
- Select a recipe and read it carefully. (This can be a shared reading activity.)
- Explain instructions in recipes, for instance 'Crack egg on side of bowl and empty into mixture.' 'Add egg to mixture' could result in the shell being added as well!
- Make sure you have everything you need before you start.
- Take your time. Do not hurry in the kitchen.
- Measure ingredients carefully. Talk together about different measures.
- Always taste the food you are cooking. Enjoy the smells!
- Keep a broom handy and sweep up everything you drop.
- Wash up. Put everything away when you have finished.

A Grandparent Golden Hint

Give plenty of encouragement and praise.

Cooking for the family

Teach your grandchildren to cook dishes to make later for their family. Venture away from the safe old standards such as chocolate crackles and biscuits. Why not try coq au vin, bread-making, chocolate souffle or pumpkin soup?

A Grandparent Golden Cooking Hint

Stand back. Don't interfere too much.

Don't say 'Don't' all the time.

Presentation

Grandparents know the value of presentation. Teach your grandchildren the art of setting an attractive table which can turn the simplest meal into a celebration. Teach them how to serve with style, to take the time to serve food in an appetising way, so it not only tastes good but looks good!

A breakfast tray

Show grandchildren how to prepare a simple breakfast tray. This is always a hit with parents and special people.

Fruit juice, toast or croissants, with butter and jam in little dishes on a tray is fine. Napkins and a flower in a vase makes a special breakfast.

Older grandchildren can be taught the art of making a good cup of tea or coffee, not instant coffee and hot water from the tap, or tea with tea leaves floating on the top.

'Cold' cooking

'Cold' cooking – salads, healthy drinks, biscuits and slices which do not require cooking – is a great way to get younger grandchildren started in cooking.

'Add and stir' recipes

Simple 'Add and stir' recipes for cakes, puddings and biscuits, where ingredients are added, stirred and placed into a microwave or standard oven, are useful for young cooks.

Prepared foods

Cake mixes

Never turn your nose up at cake mixes. Many taste delicious. What's more, a good cake mix can be prepared entirely by a grandchild and adds to their cooking confidence, especially when it is enjoyed by the family.

Sauces

Prepared foods, such as tomato sauces, can be a great standby. They are appetising and can be used for pasta and other main course recipes.

Pastry

Prepared and packet pastry mixes are another great standby. Grandchildren can have lots of fun as they make their own pies, pasties, tarts and biscuits.

When they become more proficient cooks, introduce them to the art of making sauces and pastry.

Discipline

Providing supportive back-up for a family's discipline is the best way grandparents can make life easier for parents and grandchildren.

If members of a family have individual opinions and philosophies on discipline it can create immeasurable difficulties. Interfering in the discipline within a family will only cause distress.

However, when grandchildren are with you in your home for short- or long-term visits, you must provide simple guidelines or discipline which will create a peaceful and secure environment for your grandchildren.

Establish clear limits and boundaries.

Rules need to be clear and specific. 'Pack the toys away before dinner' is better than 'Don't forget to clean up your mess.'

Anticipate problems before they happen.

Keep calm.

Use rewards.

Escape outside.

Put on a suitable video or play some music.

Always be ready with an olive branch.

Modern families

No longer do all families resemble the traditional family of two parents, two children and one dog. As well as traditional families there are blended families, single-parent families and families that include 'special persons' for care and support.

Grandparents, and there may be many grandparents, are only one part of the family environment – only one cog in a very big wheel.

In your own home

Grandparents all over the world will tell you that their grandchildren are angelic – an absolute delight. However, some grandchildren with gutsy little temperaments can be a bit difficult to handle – but only sometimes.

A few guidelines will help keep potential little terrorists in line when they are occupying your house. Peace, not war, is the aim.

Team Workers

Grandparents are wonderful team workers. They love to work with grandchildren in a super co-operative team.

☞ Make sure the grandchildren hear and understand your requests.

☞ Give them time to follow your instructions, and give minimum instructions at one time.

If you do this you will find it is fun to work with your team of grandchildren sharing such mundane tasks as tidying up, cooking, cleaning, etc.

A Hot Discipline Tip

Don't say anything you can't or don't want to do!

Attitude

A change in your attitude can help deal with tricky discipline situations – especially when the children are looking on.

Take a positive attitude! The right attitude can only assist your blood pressure level.

Consistency

Consistency is one of the foundations of effective child management. This is why we can't interfere in the discipline within a family because, for most grandparents, we're only occasionally on the grandchild's home base, looking on.

However, we can practise consistent discipline when grandchildren are staying with us.

Inconsistency confuses grandchildren. It teaches them not to listen. It shows our grandchildren how to manipulate us.

General discipline tips

Avoid . . .
- Problems before they happen.
- Shouting.
- Physical discipline of all kinds, that is smacking.
- Nose-to-nose confrontations and power struggles.
- Verbal baiting from older grandchildren.

Manners

It is perfectly acceptable to expect your grandchildren to use 'please' and 'thank you'. If there is a little slowness in the use of manners, model the correct responses quietly: 'Please may I have a drink.' Wait attentively until the child can offer the correct response.

Car discipline

- Only begin to drive the car when grandchildren are strapped in a car seat or secured by seat belts.
- Stop the car when children fight. Let them know you will drive only when they are quiet. This is safe for your grandchildren and safe for you.

Rewards

Grandparents have been using rewards or positive consequences since time began. A reward can be described as paying positive attention to your grandchildren, giving or doing something they like or find enjoyable when they have demonstrated good behaviour!

In giving rewards grandparents focus more on the good behaviour and less on the bad.

Hopefully, if the consequences for being good outweigh the consequences for being bad, even the most stubborn grandchild is bound to understand sooner or later!

'First do what I want, then you can do what you want!'

This particular grandparent's rule has proved popular throughout the ages, for example, 'Eat your vegetables, then you can have some dessert!'

No matter how sneaky this technique may seem, it works. It works really well when there is some type of activity involved that is of great interest to the particular grandchild

Try, 'Help Grandma clean up and we can go to the park!'

Customised Rewards!

Because there are no two grandchildren alike, rewards or positive consequences must be individualised to suit each child's individual personality.

Tantrums

Tantrums usually come in two varieties: the noisy, door slamming, floor-stomping type, or the quiet, sulking variety. Tantrums are designed to break down parent and grandparent resistance. Tantrums rarely happen when no one is around. Tantrums have a purpose and require an audience.

Remove yourself when temper tantrums occur. This is safest for your grandchild and for you.

Communicating with grandchildren

Talking is something we don't think about much – but it is something most grandparents do very well. Talking and listening are essential ingredients in a healthy relationship with grandchildren.

The quality of our conversation with our grandchildren can make a difference to their language development. When we talk to them we are giving messages at two levels – the spoken word plus the underlying messages that can help shape a grandchild's attitude to the world and the way they see themselves.

Today, when everyone is living such busy lives, talking with grandchildren can be on the run and incidental: chatting with babies and toddlers while they are being bathed, fed or dressed; talking with older grandchildren while preparing a meal or driving them in the car.

Find some time for a real conversation with grandchildren.

Remember:

Grandchildren, like us, are often tired and don't feel like communicating. They need some space and time for themselves.

Conversation tactics

☛ Meals are great social occasions. Make the most of meal times when everyone is in one place and glued to their seats.

☛ Take the lead. Share your own day. Talk about the peaks and valleys on life's journey. Laugh and talk about the worst thing that happened to you during the day.

☛ Make sure you have one-on-one time with individual grandchildren.

☛ Ask open questions, questions that begin with What . . . Where . . . How . . . and When . . . Questions such as 'What was the best thing that happened at school today?' should bring more than a one-word answer.

☛ Some grandchildren can be very difficult to get started. Remember that grandchildren, especially boys, are more likely to open up and talk if they are relaxed and taking part in an activity they enjoy. Spark up conversations on walks or when fishing, etc. Talk on the grandchild's own territory, for example in their room where they feel relaxed and secure.

Giving instructions

☛ Do not assume grandchildren will understand your instructions.

☛ Use simple language when explaining a task or giving instructions to young grandchildren.

☛ Divide a task into steps and explain one step at a time!

☛ Make sure you have the child's attention before giving instructions. Use your grandchild's name. Squat or bend to their level to get eye-to-eye attention.

☛ Be brief. The longer you talk the more your grandchildren will be at risk of becoming 'grandparent deaf'.

☛ See if children can repeat what you have said.

Giving instructions clearly

It is easy to guide and organise children if you give positive instructions clearly and explicitly.

Rather than

'Don't fall, Joanna' try 'Think about your climbing, Joanna!'

Not 'Tidy up, please Henry' but

'Help me put the toys in the basket, Henry.'

Safe, clear instructions help keep grandchildren safe.

Rather than 'I won't be able to rescue you if you fall!' use 'Hold onto your bicycle with both hands.'

'Hold my hand, Cleo, and we'll wait for the cars to go.' Giving firm simple requests with a justification makes sense to a grandchild.

'Please shut the door, Anthony – the breeze is cold on Grandma's back.'

'Don't do that, Jeffrey!' is not as effective as 'Take your foot off the cat's tail Jeffrey. It's hurting the cat.'

'I want you to be a good boy, Joe, when we are at the doctor's' is not as clear as 'When Grandma is at the doctor's I want you to be quiet and play with the toys so you don't disturb other people.'

Modelling

Modelling – that is being polite, clear, concise and attentive to people in your everyday communication – is a great way to show grandchildren how to communicate with people they meet in everyday life.

Be Positive!

Think about telling grandchildren what to do rather than what **not** to do.

Communication hints

- ☞ Make your grandchildren offers they can't resist, for example 'If you get dressed quickly we'll go to the park.'
- ☞ Be positive: 'We walk inside the house. We run outside the house.'
- ☞ Don't yell.
- ☞ If you lose your cool, be prepared to back down.
- ☞ Give choices (but not too many at once): 'Do you want to put on your pyjamas first or brush your teeth?'
- ☞ Give and take. 'You can't go to the shops on your own but you can play in the garden by yourself.'

Perceiving can be deceiving! Points of view

The way you see a situation can be completely different from your grandchildren's view of the same situation.

Always be prepared to listen to a grandchild's point of view and explain further. For instance you see Tyrone as being very dirty and in desperate need of a bath. Tyrone can see that only half of him is dirty and he needs a wash – not a bath.

Challenging arguments

It is possible to be challenging and argue with an older grandchild. A good challenging argument can help older grandchildren clarify their thinking. Just make sure you don't dominate. Give time for their side of the argument.

Taxi-ing grandchildren

Grandparents often help with taxi-ing grandchildren to and from school and to and from other activities. Take this opportunity to talk and discuss things in general with grandchildren.

'Ping-ponging'

Avoid ping-ponging between grandparents, that is, 'Go and ask your grandmother – Go and ask your grandfather.' Don't let your grandchildren play one grandparent against another.

Some don'ts

☛ Don't use guilt to control grandchildren when you communicate with them, for example 'Look what you have done to Grandma. She's exhausted!'

☛ Avoid frightening threats, for example 'If you pull a face like that the wind will change and you will stay like it!'

☛ Don't put grandchildren down. Think carefully about pet names for grandchildren. Some, such as 'Dumbo' or 'Bones', can hurt and stay with a child through a lifetime!

Keeping secrets

It is impossible to keep secrets from grandchildren. Children know everything about everything – and everyone. And don't think if you tell them a secret they will keep it from their parents. Discuss problems clearly, simply and openly if families are going through a rough patch.

Changes in behaviour

If a grandchild seems quieter or develops into a little pain, something out of the ordinary could be happening. A parent may be ill, a marriage could be going through a shaky stage, or affections are having to be shared with the arrival of a new baby. Allow your grandchildren space to discuss how they feel. Listening can be a marvellous beginning to solving many problems.

Telephone tactics

The telephone, message machines, faxes and the computer are vital communication lifelines for grandparents. Telephone calls to friends and for professional reasons are important for our well-being!

Before an invasion of grandchildren, take steps to safeguard your communication equipment. Remove it to a safe place – out of reach of small fingers.

Talking on the phone

You can guarantee that young grandchildren will want your attention the minute the phone rings or you need to make a call!

☛ To distract a grandchild while you are making an important call have a snack ready, a bag full of safe and interesting bits and pieces, or their own toy telephone, to keep them occupied.

☛ Fasten the phone so it cannot be taken off the hook to leave you without a connection.

Grandparenting from a distance

Many grandparents and their grandchildren live far from each other. Connect and communicate by means of little 'stay-in-touch' notes, letters, faxes, telephone calls or 'e-mail'.

Keep grandchildren informed about what you are doing. Ask them to tell you the best things that have happened to them recently.

Breaks in family relationships

Grandparents are normal mortals. They are quite capable of blowing their fuse and losing their cool. This can happen at any time.

Apologise if you're in the wrong. No one is perfect. Listen and be tolerant. It's a different world from when we were young. Work hard to mend your relationship with the family even if it appears that the effort is all one way. Don't over-indulge with material possessions to ease your guilt. Go gently, be persistent. Grandparents know that persistence pays off in the long run.

Handy Grandparent Hint

Caution

Grandparents need to be careful of anything said in haste or under pressure. A spur-of-the-moment comment, combined with a raised voice and stern look, can scare young grandchildren. Remember too, a grandchild's interpretation can often be faulty. Elaborate if you are greeted by a puzzled, unsure look.

Keep a diary of special events coming up in your grandchildren's lives – speech nights, school performances, birthdays, sports finals, etc.

Telling young grandchildren about storks or fairies bringing babies rarely works today! And it is misleading!

Answering questions

Grandchildren have the happy knack of asking questions, out of the blue, that can knock the socks off you.

For run-of-the-mill questions young children need short, simple, factual answers.

If they need more information, they will ask for it.

For older children, a good reply is, 'I'm not sure of that, Cynthia. Let's find out. We'll use the encyclopedia (CD Rom, whatever)'.

Difficult and tricky questions

Grandchildren have a talent for asking difficult and tricky questions. Tricky questions are usually about sex. Remember, a grandparent's aim in life is not to rock the boat. Harmony with parents and support for their viewpoints in bringing up their children is important.

However, you can use all your diplomatic skills to disagree with the way parents deal with their children's difficult and tricky questions. 'Knowledge is power' is a persuasive argument if you feel parents should be more forthcoming in answering children's questions.

Knowledge can provide self-protection and self-preservation for children.

Room at the inn?

'Can you squeeze us in? I know it's short notice but . . .'

You reply, 'Of course we can, dear?' Then comes the panic.

How and where can you squeeze a family of three, four or more – parents and of course the adorable grandchildren – into your home, which usually accommodates one or two adults and a pet or two?

The thing to remember is not to panic. Be creative.

Stretch the imagination. Imagine your home's floor plan is flexible. The office can be moved into your bedroom. The dining and sitting rooms can become bedrooms, etc., etc.

Borrow or buy extra mattresses and other equipment from friends.

'Room at the inn' handy hints

☞ Call in extra help. Get assistance to help move furniture.

☞ Arrange for separate sleeping spaces for older and younger grandchildren. (Older grandchildren usually like to stay up later to chat or read in bed, younger grandchildren should go to bed early!)

☞ Keep your own private space, even if your bedroom is crowded with office, art and craft, fishing or golf equipment. Don't give up your bedroom at any cost. You will need a sanctuary.

☞ Set up a few rules to maintain order and consideration for guests and hosts. Knock, and wait to be invited into a room, share chores, don't monopolise the bathroom, etc.

☞ Allocate a 'quiet' space in your home. Everyone needs some quiet space where they can reflect, resolve problems, gather resources or just daydream!

☞ Safety-proof your outside environment. It's a good idea if you can set aside a space for grandchildren to have some solitude for quiet play.

On the other hand . . . be prepared to say 'No' to excessive demands on your time and home.

Saying 'No' can be the best response when you are feeling stretched and stressed.

Avoiding chaos

Making a mess is a skill that some children develop early in their little lives. Within the one family, one grandchild can be orderly and love things to be neat, another a charming but dazzling clutter-bug who adores chaos.

By adopting a few sensible house rules, life will be easier when grandchildren – and their parents – stay with you. Expect children to be responsible in the nicest possible way.

House rules

A few house rules and gentle reminders about helping out and pulling their weight is a realistic expectation, adjusted to the age of the grandchildren, of course.

You want grandchildren to be relaxed and happy in your home. This does not mean they have permission to jump all over your furniture and cause other chaos.

A simple list of house rules, negotiated with your grandchildren, will keep you sane.

Sanity rules

- ☑ Place dirty clothes in the dirty-clothes basket.
- ☑ Do not enter or play in 'no-go' zones, for example your study, or the dining room adorned with precious ornaments.
- ☑ Keep toys in the toy box or basket. Expect grandchildren to pack up toys after they have finished. Give a reminder. Help younger children with this task.
- ☑ Meals will be eaten at the table.
- ☑ TV viewing will be for agreed programs and times.
- ☑ Make sure grandchildren know where to put food scraps, rubbish or unwanted articles.
- ☑ Chores will be done as a team. There should be no comments such as 'I didn't make the mess!'
- ☑ Pets are to be treated with respect and kindness.
- ☑ Belongings and clothes will not be spread all over the house.

Turn off the TV or shut down other distractions. Give five-minute warnings.

Responsibility

Allocate a sleeping area and place for each grandchild's suitcase and belongings. These areas will be the responsibility of the grandchild.

Reasonable responsibilities

☞ Encourage older grandchildren to prepare their own healthy between-meal snacks. Expect the kitchen to be left in the same state as it was found.

☞ Turn lights off when leaving a room empty.

☞ Limit telephone calls – even local ones.

☞ If you have limited hot water, use a timer and expect users to stick to a set time when showering.

☞ If you have limited bathroom space, use a timer for bathroom use.

☞ Discourage 'I want'. Encourage 'I would like . . .' or 'May I . . .'

☞ Advise grandchildren to leave the room and find another activity, for example reading, if there is squabbling and arguing over minor matters.

Self-help is wonderful

It is easy for parents to develop the habit of doing everything for children because, with busy lifestyles, it can be quicker and can save time.

Usually grandparents have plenty of time. When grandchildren are staying with you, you can work with them and help them on the road to becoming resourceful, capable human beings.

Self-help tips for grandchildren = sanity for grandparents

- ☛ Encourage and make it easy for grandchildren to get their own breakfast.
- ☛ Allow children to plan, prepare and cook some meals when they stay with you.
- ☛ Teach older children how to use your microwave and the washing machine.
- ☛ Show older children how to iron, mend and alter their own clothes.
- ☛ Can younger grandchildren tell the time? Teach them to use an alarm clock. Negotiate a reasonable hour for getting up and going to bed when they stay with you.

Being bored is cool!

It is cool for grandchildren to be bored in your house. This gives them the opportunity to find something to entertain themselves.

Being boring allows grandparents time off from entertaining grandchildren, and encourages children to develop their own creative initiative.

Reward charts . . .

- ☑ Make a simple reward chart when grandchildren come to stay.
- ☑ Keeping the house tidy = a tick
- ☑ Two ticks = a star
- ☑ A star = a treat.
- ☑ (Rewards could be money to spend or take home, or small gifts. The treat could also be an activity you have already chosen to do.)

Teenage grandchildren

Adolescence can be the worst of times – even in the best of families. But grandparents don't have to worry about adolescent angst or enrol in a stress management course because of teenage grandchildren. They have already survived one set of adolescent years and have an inkling of what it involves. They are prepared for mood swings, from extreme self-confidence to crippling self-doubt.

Grandparents can enjoy teenage grandchildren as friends and companions, and appreciate the pleasure and fun they bring to their lives.

In spite of contrary belief, grandparents know that most teenagers are not out to make life difficult for everyone about them. Today's world is confusing and challenging for teenagers, and grandparents can play a part in offering positive support in raising happy, well-adjusted teenagers. Let grandchildren know where you stand on issues. Be prepared to listen to their opinions too.

Boosting teenage self-esteem

The worry and pressure of peers, education, future employment, and fractured and nuclear families can provide many problems for teenagers today.

Grandparents can help build a teenage grandchild's self-esteem.

Self-esteem generates confidence so that they will be able to express themselves, as well as listen to and respect the rights of others.

Hints to build self-esteem

☞ Let grandchildren know you love and believe in them.

☞ Listen to them.

☞ Talk with them on an equal basis.

☞ Acknowledge and praise the good things they do.

☞ Include them as a valued part in your life.

☞ Have fun with them!

Conflict with teenage grandchildren

Grandparents don't need to be perfect all the time and if you find you cannot connect with a teenage grandchild, don't feel hurt and distanced.

Be truthful. Grandparents have learnt the importance of apologising when in the wrong. Clear up issues between you so that no grudges are held. Then move on.

On the other hand, don't be treated as a doormat. Do not allow your values and standards to be compromised. Remember you are a worthwhile person and have a right to be treated with respect.

Keep communication channels open so you can give support if needed. Today's teenagers rarely leave home at sixteen or seventeen and may stay on for another decade. There will be many times when you can reconnect with your grandchild and offer support, love and friendship.

To Defuse a Confrontation

Walk away and wait till things calm down.

Meet for coffee, sit down and talk about things. This is a great start to solving problems.

When teenage grandchildren visit

With clear, firm limits and boundaries in place, having teenage grandchildren to stay can be an absolute delight.

When teenage grandchildren stay with you, whether for a short or long time, you will need to negotiate and set limits and boundaries for responsible behaviour. This is a safeguard for your grandchildren.

Make sure your grandchildren realise that limits set on their behaviour expresses your concern for them. 'Tough but fair' is usually accepted by teenagers.

Negotiate as grandparent to grandchild, not adult to adult, and set consistent rules. 'Anything for a quiet life' is not the maxim grandparents should follow. If you find teenage grandchildren difficult to cope with in your own home, don't offer accommodation. Enjoy their company when you visit them in their own home.

Providing teenage grandchildren with information so they can reach sensible decisions can be as simple as using a bus time-table to resolve time-limit problems and make good decisions.

Solve potential problems with a prior meeting so grandchildren can have input into how life in your home is organised. Negotiate and agree on a few simple house rules, such as sensible noise limits on music.

Curfews for teenage grandchildren

Teenage grandchildren must stick to agreed times, prearranged, for returning home. In case of an emergency they are expected to phone you immediately. Visiting rights to grandparents will be withdrawn promptly if these house rules are not agreed to.

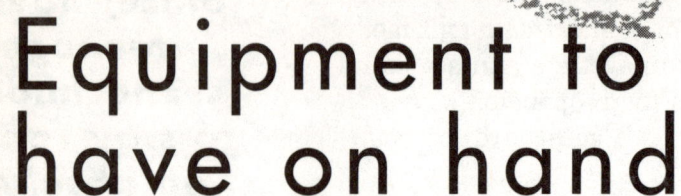

Equipment to have on hand

The list of equipment for a new grandchild can be formidable, and buying an item from this list can be a tremendous help to parents.

If you have the space, extra equipment such as cots (preferably folding), baby chairs, car seats and prams can be stored at your home. If you are buying a baby cot look for one with a certificate seal showing it meets national safety standards. Many old cots have unsafe designs and can cause accidents. If you are going to babysit on a regular basis, this can save a lot of bother.

Don't be daunted, however, by lists of equipment needed when young grandchildren come to visit. Reputable baby equipment hire firms can meet most baby needs for the short-term.

Toys, an art and craft box, a useful box, a dress-up box and some cuddly soft animals are all useful equipment for grandparents. Find out more about these in 'Things to Do', Part 2, page 171. A sandpit and paddling pool also can be included as essential equipment for young grandchildren.

Sharing

Very young grandchildren are not capable of understanding the idea of sharing. Avoid problems by having plenty of equipment such as paint, brushes and paper for everyone.

Don't expect one grandchild to share his favourite teddy with another. Have some extra soft cuddly toys as substitutes in residence at your house.

Toys

It's a great idea to have a basic collection of toys for grandchildren to play with at your house. You can make many toys, buy them or hunt for them at markets and garage sales.

- Blocks of all shapes, sizes and colours
- Containers suitable for water or sand play
- Cars, trucks, planes and ships
- Sets of farm animals
- Plastic fences and road mats to encourage potential town planners
- Dolls, prams, tea-sets and kitchen play utensils
- Cash register and a collection of empty containers for playing shop
- Carpentry sets and doctor sets to promote role-playing

Sandpits

Sandpits make heaven-sent play areas for young grandchildren, and you don't need a large area or to redesign your garden.

☞ Use an empty paddling pool to hold the sand. You can also use an old tyre which can be bought from a wrecker or garage. Slice the top from the tyre.

☞ Stock the sandpit with plastic containers of all shapes and sizes, and buckets and spades.

☞ Cover the sandpit at night to keep animals out, and to keep it dry. An upturned bucket under the cover will stop a puddle from gathering on the cover when it is raining.

Paddling pools

Paddling pools also come under practical play equipment for grandchildren. Remember, the children will need constant supervision while they are playing in a paddling pool.

Set up the pool on grass rather than cement or concrete – it will be less slippery underfoot.

Put a basin of water beside the pool so children can step into it before getting into the pool. This will keep the pool free of grass and dirt.

A survival guide to prams

Grandparents know the main aim of walking a grandchild in a pram is to escape into the fresh air – away from the pressures of four walls – out into the wider world with all its distractions.

Grandparents also know that the gentle bumping rhythm that comes from walking or rocking a pram will send a grandchild to sleep.

On wheels with grandchildren

A pram, pusher or stroller is a great convenience item and important equipment for grandparents.

The 'nanny' style pram is still available for gentle strolls in parks, but the modern pram has undergone many changes. Prams today have to meet stringent safety regulations, work efficiently on a variety of surfaces, and fold to be taken on public transport or carried in the boot of the family car, as well as having somewhere to fit the shopping. Some prams even have a space on the end for an older toddler to sit.

Caution!

A grandparent's offer to buy a pram can sometimes break the budget. Some prams approach the cost of an international sports car!

Hints for buying prams

☞ Consult the family before racing off to buy the equivalent of a Rolls Royce or Ferrari model pram. The type of pram your family prefers will depend on their lifestyle.

☞ Beware of pram showroom salespeople. When they see a grandparent as a customer their sales attack can be similar to used car salespeople!

☞ Don't be deceived by pretty, cute prams. Look for light and practical construction, a well-made pram which will give you value for money.

☞ Some prams can convert to stroller, pusher-style prams with extra fittings.

☞ Check the wheel size. Large wheels make pushing easier, wider tyres ride over bumps well. However, small wheels make a neat folding package. Check that wheels swivel. Good suspension gives the child a pleasant ride.

☞ Look for a high baby-carrying section so that it is not as far to bend to reach the new baby.

☞ Most of the frame that can be reached by the child should be padded so little fingers cannot get hurt.

☞ Complete weather protection is important – check to ensure protection gear will fit tightly against wind and rain.

☞ Look for prams that are strong but light and easy to fold down.

☞ Steel prams are strong but heavier to lift. Aluminium and plastic prams are lighter to lift and fold, although plastic prams usually have a shorter life.

☞ Check the size of the pram when folded. Will it fit into the family's or your own car? Remember the back seat of a car will be taken up by a baby capsule.

☞ Shopping trays and a seat for toddlers are often extra fittings.

Driving the pram

☛ Practise collapsing the pram until you can do it quickly and efficiently before setting off.

☛ Check out the brakes on the pram. Always use the brakes when you stop. Chasing a runaway pram is a bit tricky.

☛ Check that the flap at the foot of the pram is fastened. Be careful that the baby does not slide down the pram with the movement as you stride along.

☛ Once a baby can sit up, make sure they are strapped in.

☛ Check your route. If going to a department store make sure you know where the lifts, toilets and restaurants are. Facing long flights of stairs with a pram is no joke. Make sure you know how long it will take to get to your destination; you may have to return quickly with a distressed grandchild.

☛ Pack supplies: tissues or wipes, spare nappy and a spare bottle of milk or water. Take a thermos flask, snack and reading matter if walking to the park.

☛ Park the pram at your nearest friendly outdoor cafe and enjoy a drink and snack.

☛ Be a careful pram driver. Watch out for pedestrians on the pavements, especially dawdlers. A bump to the ankles from a pram can be painful!

☛ Cross roads with caution.

☛ Beware! Taking a toddler and/or the family pet for a stroll, with the baby in a pram, requires super energy and control, and could result in a minor disaster.

☛ Mind that you don't overload the pram with shopping so it becomes unbalanced and tips over.

Grandparents Golden Rule

Never leave a baby unattended in a pram.

A survival kit for grandparent visits

It's a good idea to have a survival kit ready to pick up and go when you are called out on emergency visits or go for overnight stays with your grandchildren.

Footwear

Don't laugh. Comfortable shoes and/or boots, and good quality socks, are much underrated essential items of equipment for grandparents. 'Age-enhanced' feet can be very temperamental.

Being with grandchildren usually entails long hours on your feet. Skimping on good quality footwear is not an option.

Walking boots

Good quality boots are absolutely necessary if grandparents have any aspirations to walk any distance and especially to walk in the wild. Nothing is worse than finding yourself grounded for a couple of days to recover from blisters, or having to continue in spite of the pain you are suffering.

Try to buy boots in advance of departure on a big trip. Wear them in before you begin even short walking trips.

Choose your walking boots wisely. Look for boots that are durable and waterproof.

Don't forget to buy good quality hiking socks. They will minimise blisters and make life a lot more comfortable.

The sleeping bag

The sleeping bag can be a useful and important piece of equipment for grandparents. It can be a source of comfort on journeys to far-away places or when staying in the family's home.

Sleeping bags come in all shapes and sizes, weights, season gradings, fills and fill weights, fabrics and designs. Even the number of zips in a bag will determine how versatile and useful it can be in the middle of the night, in strange homes or unusual weather conditions.

The sleeping bag you invest in will depend on whether you are a warm sleeper, the areas you will be likely to visit and personal taste. Will you sleep better in a bag filled with goose down or synthetic filling?

Grandparents Handy Tip

Always travel with band-aids in your bag or wallet when out and about.

Grandparents Essential Technology

Many grandparents find mobile phones, faxes, computers, a walkman or discman invaluable equipment. You must include these in your luggage if they have become an essential part of your daily life.

Sheets and sleeping mat

- ☞ You will need sleeping sheets for sleeping bags. Silk is lighter than cotton.
- ☞ A sleeping mat provides comfort when you are sleeping on the ground or floor.

An emergency insulation blanket is handy if you travel through snow or stay in adverse weather conditions, such as the open-plan lounge room of the family home.

Learning with grandparents

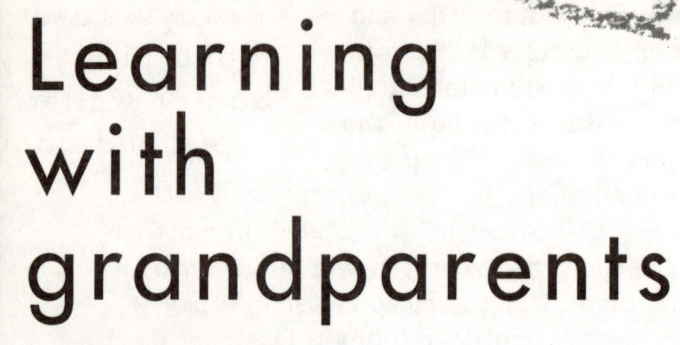

Take care that your grandchildren do not see you in the role of a traditional school teacher. However, if you are, or have been, a teacher this can be a bit tricky.

The secret is to make any activity as much fun as possible and to keep the pressure off. Grandchildren should never feel that they have to 'work' when they are with you.

Provide plenty of free play time and space for them to learn through play and discovery. Allow young grandchildren to play freely with a variety of objects.

When you are working at home, or are involved in activities out and about, you can pass on information to older grandchildren, but always do it in a cheerful and natural way.

Grandparents can provide unique opportunities to communicate, and to introduce and connect grandchildren to different interests and cultures.

Incidental learning

☛ Encourage grandchildren to ask questions and to observe what they see around them.

☛ Discuss the history and physical features of places you visit. Ask questions such as 'Why do you think some houses have chimneys?'

☛ When you travel in trains ask questions such as 'How many different kinds of roofs can you see?'

☛ Older grandchildren may be able to come up with answers to questions such as 'Why do you think there is a fish cannery in this town?'

A quiet-time device

A scrapbook is a great quiet-time device to use when you and young grandchildren need a break.

Help them make and keep a scrapbook. Fill the book or books with souvenirs – for example train tickets, brochures, and other mementoes of their visit with you. Use pictures cut from magazines and newspapers as well as photographs. Young grandchildren can dictate their writing to you. They can draw the pictures.

Keep the scrapbook at your house as an on-going record of their time spent with you.

A daily diary

Writing a daily diary is a great way to help older grandchildren keep up their reading and writing skills.

Grandchildren can write an entry each day when they visit or stay with you. Even on days when there are no trips or great excitement, they can write about meals and the weather.

Keep a diary in your home for each grandchild or buy a notebook they can take home with them.

Finished entries can be read out for the family to enjoy.

Spelling

☛ Don't make too much of grandchildren's incorrect spelling.

☛ Quickly help your grandchild to correct the words.

☛ Slip in an odd spelling rule that may help.

☛ Praise the creativity and ideas within their writing.

Reading

Reading aloud and telling stories will help promote listening skills, extend children's vocabulary, reinforce language structures and spark imaginations.

☛ Join the local library and allow grandchildren to select their own books for quiet times such as evenings or rainy days.

☛ Serial reading, reading aloud a chapter each day, is a lovely way to encourage grandchildren's love of literature.

☛ Reading maps is an important skill children can use when they travel with you. Mark off distances covered, towns, rivers and other geographical features. This activity can help ward off the unending question, 'Are we nearly there?'

Maths

Grandchildren will love record-keeping tasks. When travelling by car, the cost of petrol, distance travelled, estimated time of arrival and speed involved make interesting maths activities. Averages and totals can be calculated and discussed.

When you involve grandchildren in budgeting, such as giving them an allowance from which they must cover their expenses, it makes for great incidental maths learning.

For younger grandchildren simple maths activities can be found inside and outside your home. Encourage counting and limiting numbers by asking a grandchild to count cutlery as they set the table.

You can help young grandchildren understand concepts such as more, less, bigger and smaller by observing different objects in the kitchen.

Encourage grandchildren to budget for an expensive day by cutting back on other days.

Music

Introduce grandchildren not only to your favourite music but to a variety of music styles.

With younger grandchildren you can make simple rhythm instruments and encourage them to move to the beat. Saucepan lids, wooden spoons and plastic containers filled with uncooked rice or dried beans make wonderful rhythm accompaniments.

Family games are important, and great learning tools. They also teach grandchildren to share and co-operate. Grandparents know that card games are one of the best learning tools ever invented.

Exam time and older grandchildren

Final exams can be a stressful time for grandchildren and the family. Grandparents can support grandchildren and the family by being calm, not adding to pressure but offering encouragement.

Grandparents know from experience that obsessive study and cramming is not the most effective method to success in exams.

Failure at final exams does not mean that life is over. Good exam performance is not the only way to open doors of opportunity.

☛ Be positive. Discuss and build on successes the grandchild has achieved in and out of school.

☛ Help grandchildren to become organised in managing their time and study skills. Promote a balanced approach which includes study, rest, diet, exercise and socialisation.

Grandchildren with learning difficulties

☛ Grandparents can do much to support grandchildren with learning difficulties.

☛ Find out all you can about relevant learning disabilities, support specific organisations and pass the information on to the family.

☛ Help your grandchild know that success is possible no matter how small.

☛ Encourage special interests to build a feeling of success.

☛ Be smiling, confident and relaxed when helping your grandchild.

Let's read

Books remind us of very special moments in our childhood. Who can remember reading beneath the blankets with a torch?

Share your favourite books with your grandchildren. They can play an important part in connecting the children to your past.

Shared reading

- ☞ Read aloud to young grandchildren. Share reading aloud with older grandchildren – they read a page or chapter, you read the next.
- ☞ Buy books as gifts for your grandchildren. Borrow books from the library with them. Help grandchildren to discover the imaginative and real world around them through books.

Reading aloud

Reading aloud to your grandchildren can be one of the most rewarding experiences for grandparents.

All you need to involve your grandchild in the joys of reading:
- ☞ A comfortable, quiet spot
- ☞ A cosy reading position for two
- ☞ Some favourite books.

Children can learn about books long before they can read. Every time a story is read to them a young grandchild will gain an understanding of what a book is and how it works.

As they grow older grandchildren will gain from encounters with characters, conversations and plots from within the pages of books.

Picture story books

Picture story books are for everyone. Your grandchildren will gain pleasure from the illustrations and learn that pictures can help them understand the story.
- ☞ Encourage grandchildren to ask questions and comment about the pictures.
- ☞ Choose bright and appealing picture books to hold a pre-reader's attention. Illustrations in a picture story book should add to, as well as complement, written words.
- ☞ Board books are excellent for young grandchildren. They are easy to hold and manipulate and will help them to learn the skills of using books.

Reading grandchildren

When grandchildren are learning to read at school they like to have books other than school books to read. Grandparents can help by building a library or borrowing books from their library.

Repetition is never a worry for new readers. Books that can be read over and over again will give grandchildren a sense of achievement.

As grandchildren's reading skills improve they like to progress to 'real' books, short fiction books that are represented in chapters.

As grandchildren continue with reading they will begin to gain confidence. Confident readers enjoy books with larger amounts of text but still lots of illustrations. Illustration is still useful because it gives clues to understanding difficult words as well as the context and flow of a story.

☛ Try not to interrupt reading that is flowing to correct a misread word. Remember grandchildren will be reading for meaning. They will also be bringing their own experiences and knowledge to their understanding of the text.

☛ If a grandchild reads 'jumped' instead of 'hopped' in 'The rabbit hopped over the grass', meaning has been maintained. If the paragraph, page or book is short, wait until the end to help your grandchild recognise the correct word.

If your grandchild is making too many mistakes you will need to find an easier book so they can succeed in their reading.

Helping grandchildren read

Helping grandchildren develop into readers is a satisfying job for grandparents. To succeed in most things today, children need to read!

Pause, prompt and praise

Pause for about eight seconds before you prompt. This is an excellent strategy to give grandchildren time to use their new reading skills.

Prompts can be:

☛ Asking, 'What is the first sound of the word? What are other sounds in the word?'
☛ Looking at the size and shape of the word, using the picture cue.
☛ Rereading the sentence.
☛ Asking, 'Does that make sense? Does that sound right? Does that look right?'
☛ Share reading aloud to give your grandchild a cue to the meaning of the words and flow of the story.
☛ Don't forget! Give lots of **praise** to grandchildren for their efforts.

Discover the joys of computers

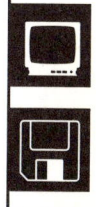

Today computers are recognised as the modern way to communicate.

Most grandchildren will be better informed about computers and technology than their grandparents. If you haven't already, why not launch off into Cyberspace? Explore the electronic world with your grandchildren. Combine a grandparent's wisdom, worldly experience and knowledge with a grandchild's techno energy and passion. Use computers in a fun, positive way.

Why not 'go techno'?

Join a friendly computer-user group. They have product demonstrations and provide training sessions. Choose a group where there is plenty of time to drink coffee and discuss computer problems and tricks.

Your local library can be a great starting point to learn about computers. Most libraries have computers available for public access and training facilities.

There are also coffee shops and other commercial facilities where you can use the Internet.

Surfing the net

'Surfing the net' is taking advantage of the computer's capacity as a communication tool. 'Surfing the net' is when you visit and explore sites on the Internet through telephone lines accessed by your computer. New friendships and contacts can be made and maintained. Information can be swapped, interests shared.

Chatting on-line

Chatting on-line is an interactive way for you to communicate via the computer. Everyone can participate and receive a reply.

Keep in touch with travelling older grandchildren or grandchildren who live across the world through e-mail.

Grandchildren who rarely talk much face-to-face can become active communicators when chatting on-line.

Computer terms

CD-ROMS

CD-ROMS look like audio CDs (small round discs) but carry text and images as well as sound. Many wonderful reference tools such as world famous encyclopaedias come in CD-ROM form as well as exciting games for grandchildren to play.

Internet

Internet is a global network of computers connecting more than 40 million users. It is used to transfer files and to publish information in the form of text, images, sound and video. The Internet is accessed by users of personal computers over a normal phone line.

World Wide Web

World Wide Web is that part of the Internet which presents information in the form of multimedia, combining text, images, sound and video. It is accessed with a web browser, such as Netscape, Navigator or Microsoft Internet Explorer.

E-mail

Messages can be sent and received via the Internet. Normally e-mail consists of text but is able to carry images and computer files. Users can key-in or type messages to each other on screen.

Home Page

A Home Page is a site or a personal collection of electronic pages on the Internet.

Web browser

Web browser is a window-like program that displays the contents of electronic pages of the web.

Using the Internet

The quality and quantity of information available through the computer, at the press of a button, is unimaginable. The information comes not only in text, but in pictures and sound and video. It is a two-way 'interactive' form of communication.

The Internet gives you access to just about any kind of information you could ever need. It's like having access to an enormous library open all hours. Using the Internet allows grandparents to do their own thing in their own time.

Sitting at the computer

Posture

Watch how you sit and use your body at the computer. Sit upright and don't stay in the same position too long. When hands are at the keyboard, the elbows should be at roughly 90-degree angles and close to the body. This means the keyboard should be close by and low enough to keep the arms parallel to the board and the wrists in the straight 'neutral' position.

Keep at least one background light on and sit about one metre from the screen.

Take breaks!

All computer users need to take breaks from the screen and keyboard.

Have a drink. Do some stretching exercises and rest the grey matter.

Mouse information

The mouse is an attachment to the computer that allows you to move text and graphics around the screen by clicking and pressing a button.

The ideal position for the mouse is on the same plane as the keyboard and as close to the keyboard as possible. The arm shouldn't be constantly extended to use the mouse.

Check the manual for instructions on cleaning the mouse and keep your mouse pad clean.

There is a variety of designs and sizes of 'mouses'. Choose a mouse that fits your hand, then you will not over-exert your hand when clicking the button. Watch out for expensive mice with buttons that are hard to push.

Computers in daily life

Computers can help you as grandparents to enhance your daily lives. You can:

- ☛ Buy, sell, be entertained, informed, browse, sample files, listen to music, listen to and watch videos.
- ☛ Gain access to famous libraries and museums all over the world.
- ☛ Plan and book holidays.
- ☛ Write letters faster.
- ☛ Keep track of shares and investments.
- ☛ Record and order family trees.
- ☛ Write a blockbuster novel.
- ☛ Connect to the Internet to communicate with friends and relatives around the world.
- ☛ Accompany older grandchildren on an overseas trip by following their progress from city to city via the World Wide Web sites. This can provide textual and graphic information on each place visited.
- ☛ 'Chat' regularly with grandchildren via e-mail
- ☛ Play chess. Players can use appropriate software and key in chess plays. Chess pieces on boards, set up by the players' computers, can be physically moved.
- ☛ Communicate with like-minded overseas groups – SeniorNet.
- ☛ Play games.

Grandparents know...

Information is not valuable in itself! It should be relevant and the user should have time to interpret it.

Using computers with grandchildren

☞ Find the interests and topics that engage your grandchild. Locate and explore sites that have information about pet interests. Make sure sites are appropriate for specific age levels. Can the information be shared with parents and friends?

☞ Assist grandchildren with homework research. Help them to select relevant information. Interpret it as you work together to discover, explore and record information.

☞ Ask grandchildren to locate on-line recipes and menu advice which can be put into practice.

☞ Encourage grandchildren to develop real-time communication with 'on-line buddies' around the world. Communicating on the Net will help grandchildren to develop self-esteem and confidence.

☞ Play games. Check content of games. Many are violent and graphic and not suitable for young children.

☞ Read and share electronic books.

☞ Use the mouse to create graphics.

Leisure time together

Sharing leisure activities with grandchildren is fun! There are many opportunities such as going to live theatre, sporting events or visiting art galleries, which can provide satisfying and entertaining times for both grandchildren and grandparents.

Going to live theatre

Grandparents who love live theatre,
whether it is a play, ballet, opera or
pop concert, can share this exciting
experience with grandchildren.
Grandchildren of about six or seven
are ready for a live performance.

Select performances that specially
cater for young children for their first
experiences of live theatre.

Be sure to share your enjoyment of
the performance with the children
afterwards.

Watching sport

Grandparents are often invited to watch grandchildren play sport. As well, grandchildren will love to accompany you when you watch and support your favourite team playing.

It is vital that grandparents model the best spectator behaviour — whether you are watching grandchildren in sporting activities or sharing your favourite spectator sport with them.

Congratulate grandchildren on their play whether they win, lose or draw.

Handy hints for spectator sports

☛ Take a portable chair or stool and/or a waterproof picnic rug.
☛ Include something to read or do if it is going to be a long day, such as when grandchildren play in district competitions.
☛ Discreetly listen on the 'Walkman' to your own team's progress if involved in grandchildren's sports.
☛ Make sure you include a thermos of tea or coffee and a snack.
☛ An umbrella is useful, whether it is hot or cold.

At all times support:

Fair play;

The rules of the game;

Decisions of umpires and officials.

Visiting art galleries

A visit to an art gallery can start grandchildren on a lifetime's enjoyment.

☛ Before your visit talk about what you will see together. Fill in background information of artists and their work for older grandchildren.

☛ Keep visits short so grandchildren will look forward to further visits.

☛ See only one or two sections of large galleries at a visit.

☛ Watch out for exhibits, special guided tours and activities that will appeal to young children.

☛ Visit gallery shops. Buy postcards and prints of favourite artwork so grandchildren can begin their own art collection.

☛ Make sure grandchildren know the rules – No touching! No running! – and why the rules are necessary.

☛ Talk about the paintings and artwork you see with them: Which do they like the best? Do they think there is a story connected to the painting? How do they think the artist painted it? etc.

Your grandchild's viewpoint on art will bring you new and fascinating perspectives.

Giving gifts . . .

It is always a thrill to watch the delight in a grandchild's eyes as they unwrap your gift. However, buying gifts for your grandchildren can be confusing. It can often mean wandering aimlessly around shopping malls and toy shops, desperately trying to find something the grandchildren will love.

Overwhelming marketing push from the commercial world of toys does nothing to dispel your confusion.

Caution!

No matter if toys are on the 'Top 10 Must-have List' for grandchildren, avoid them like poison if you feel they have the potential to give you a nervous breakdown.

If they are to be kept at your family's home, and the family are agreeable, that's a different story. Such toys could be water cannons and pistols, trucks with sirens, dolls with a very limited vocabulary, whistles, drums and other musical instruments.

The power of magazine and television advertising can set many a grandchild's heart on toys that grandparents wouldn't choose themselves. So you need to walk a fine line. You must strike a balance between bringing joy and pleasure, avoiding toys you don't like without causing disappointment, and getting good value for money!

'Cool' gifts!

Grandparents know the power of popular culture and the influence of the mass market. They remember and understand how cruel the world can seem if you are not part of it. They can relate to a twelve-year-old's desires to be 'cool' and in with their peers.

Today's world of IT (information technology) and popular culture can leave grandparents floundering and in a whirl of confusion. What's hot this year? Who is who? What is what? What do grandchildren want? Will the grandchildren like 'on-selling' merchandise?

Have faith that grandchildren will love traditional, wrapped-up surprises and that you are the perfect person to give them.

No matter what the gift-giving pressures are around us, you should never lose the concept of unconditional gift-giving – giving a grandchild a special token of affection.

Guidelines for buying gifts . . .

☛ Think about each individual grandchild, their interests, age and capabilities.

☛ Be aware of the grandchild's development level. If in doubt, ask shop assistants about the appropriateness of a toy.

☛ Consult with the family, but if you disagree with their recommendations, or the price is out of your range, forget it. Take your own gift buying path.

☛ Select gifts that encourage the creative use of the imagination such as farm sets, dolls' houses, dress-ups and craft packages.

☛ Avoid toys that leave nothing to the imagination. Some toys literally walk, talk, say what they need and what to do with them.

☛ Using games and sporting equipment can help develop communication and social skills such as taking turns, sharing and co-operating. When buying such items take into consideration that they usually require more than one person to play.

☛ Providing grandchildren with a diversity of experiences is a factor to consider. For example, buy an outdoor toy if the child spends a lot of time at the computer.

☛ Avoid toys that enforce sexism, racism or violence. The classic 'violent' toy is the gun. Sometimes it can be difficult to discourage grandchildren from playing with such toys but *you* do not have to buy them.

☛ Don't forget that girls need and enjoy the experience of constructing things, just as boys need and enjoy the experience of playing with toys that encourage domestic play such as tea sets, dolls, dress-ups and model kitchen equipment.

Gift ideas

The sky is the limit and the variety of toys available for grandchildren is unending.

Handy grandparents are just the right people to be able to sew or build gifts, such as dress-ups, sand pits, cubby houses and other suitable play furniture.

Gather together craft materials for writing kits. Depending on the materials you include they will suit grandchildren of all ages. A useful box or writing kit could contain crayons, pencils, paints, adhesive tape, assortment of writing paper, glue and scissors.

Writing kits for older children could consist of folders, envelopes, writing paper and pens, staplers, folders, Blu-tac and paper clips, glue and scissors.

Jewellery, watches, and T-shirts are popular gift ideas for older grandchildren.

Beach equipment such as buckets, spades, watering cans, sieves, rakes, funnels, sand castle moulds, etc. will suit young as well as older grandchildren for sand sculpting.

More gift ideas

- Musical instruments
- Sporting equipment such as a cricket bat 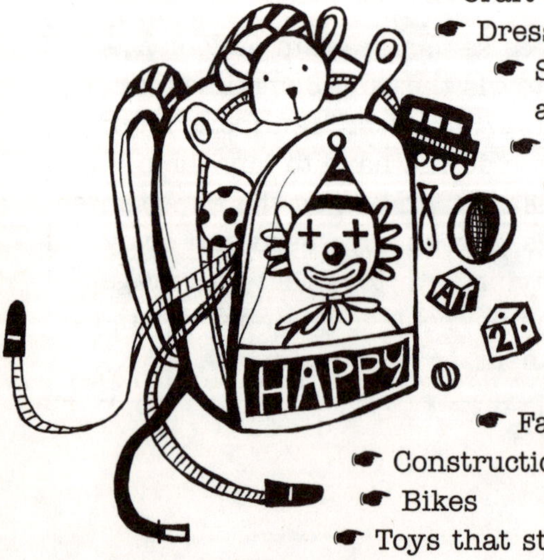
  - Craft activities
  - Dress-ups
    - Science equipment such as a magnifying glass
    - Books
      - Games
      - Puzzles
      - Stickers
        - Dolls
          - Puppets
        - Soft cuddly toys
      - Farm sets
    - Construction toys
    - Bikes
      - Toys that stack or thread
  - Bath toys
- Wooden skittle sets
- Blackboard easel, chalk and a duster

Age appropriate toys

You need to make sure that the toy is appropriate for the age and stage of development of your respective grandchildren.

Under six months – Toys for grandchildren this age should be durable and easy to clean, such as washable soft toys, rattles and mobiles.They should have no detachable parts that could be put into the mouth, nostrils or ears.

Six to twelve months – At this age baby grandchildren can crawl or pull and reach up to furniture, stand or walk. Toddlers have poor balance and fall easily. Everything touched still goes from the hand to the mouth.

Select gifts such as bath toys, nests of cubes, blocks, mobiles and cuddly toys.

One to two years – Toddling grandchildren will be exploring and seeing how things work. Nearly everything still goes into the mouth.

Select gifts such as building blocks, ride-on toys, push-along and pull-along toys, posting boxes, picture books, lightweight balls, buckets and spades.

Four to five years – Grandchildren now have acquired co-ordination and continue social and language development.

Select gifts such as simple games, paints, modelling clay and plasticene, dominoes, musical instruments and illustrated picture books, as well as story books that can be read aloud by parents.

Five to six years – Grandchildren will be exploring, climbing, riding and enjoying games at this age.

Select gifts such as kites, sewing and craft kits, carpentry kits, word or number games, swings with rubber seats, simple board games and puzzles.

When in doubt
give from the
heart!

Pets as gifts

Giving a young grandchild a cuddly puppy or kitten can be a wonderful gift, but it could also be disastrous for the puppy or kitten, and the child's family.

Check first with the family. Do they want their child to have a pet?

Have they a secure place to keep it? Are they willing to give the care a pet requires. Remember the care of a pet will fall on the parents' shoulders — not the young grandchild.

In the case of older grandchildren, if the family is happy for a child to receive a pet as a gift, prepare your grandchild for the responsibility of caring for it.

Pets are a life-long responsibility. They need regular food, water, a safe place to sleep, exercise. They also need recommended medical care, such as vaccinations, and regular medication to prevent infestations of worms etc.

Don't toy with danger!!

Toys we give to our grandchildren need to be safe! Toys for young grandchildren need to stand up to being dropped, twisted, pulled and bitten!

- ☛ Read labels and buy non-flammable, non-toxic toys.
- ☛ Do not buy explosive or projectile toys.
- ☛ Look for information on how to use the toy and any safety equipment required.
- ☛ Dispose of packaging carefully.
- ☛ Keep young children away from older grandchildren's toys that may be dangerous for them.
- ☛ Teach children how to use toys — especially bikes — correctly and safely.
- ☛ Watch for small parts that could break or come off and be swallowed or inhaled by babies at the 'anything-goes-into-the-mouth stage' or under three-year-old grandchildren.

In the garden

Grandparents who are passionate, ardent gardeners know well the joy and satisfaction they gain from a session of gardening. For grandchildren the garden can also be a place where they relax, learn to nurture things and have fun as they work with you.

In a sticky situation, an escape to the garden will make you and your grandchildren feel better.

Sensory delights

The garden is a wonderful place for grandchildren to use their senses. Introduce them to the sights, smells, sounds, touch and the taste of your garden.

Stop and listen to the sounds in your garden: birds twittering, cicadas chirping, bees buzzing and leaves rustling in the wind. Take time with grandchildren to inhale the lovely smells of your garden.

Enjoy and observe the colour, shape and size of flowers and leaves. Sit quietly and follow a trail of ants toiling away diligently.

Admire cobwebs early in the morning when the dew is on them. Watch as particular flowers fold their petals and close up for the night.

Parks and pot plants

Non-garden-owning grandparents, for example those who live in smaller accommodation spaces (which is a good thing and not to be knocked) should not panic and feel desperate at being in a gardenless state.

Parks can provide the same feelings of relaxation and well-being and bring grandchildren close to the sounds and smells of nature. So take time to visit your local gardens and parks.

Pot plants are heaven sent for grandparents who want to give grandchildren the opportunity to grow plants without too much fuss or expense.

A cautionary note

Gardening with grandchildren can rate highly as a terrifying experience if you have the kind of garden that is open during Gardening Week and is a wonder and joy to all who view it.

Grandchildren will not garden as you do. Grandchildren have different gardening goals from their grandparents. When young grandchildren finish gardening they will usually have a large amount of your garden on them, including pockets of prize plants, dug-up seedlings, etc.

Grandchildproof gardens

Take a few precautions to grandchildproof your garden and you will find electric fences are not necessary!

☛ A slight barrier is often all that is needed to protect precious garden beds, for example defining plant borders will help children realise it is a flower bed.

☛ Stake small shrubs – but make sure stakes are safe for children.

☛ Talk to your grandchildren. Explain how precious your plants are and that they need loving care – just like grandchildren.

Gardening for children

Tailor your gardening activities so it becomes gardening *for* grandchildren – not *with* grandchildren. Gardening for grandchildren can be divided into long-term or short-term outcomes.

Long-term gardening outcomes

If your grandchildren are regular visitors to your garden, you can give them a patch of garden. They can sow seeds and seedlings and watch as they develop and grow.

Short-term gardening outcomes

Short-term gardening outcomes are just as much fun. You can help children establish their own plant in a pot and take it home with them. Follow the plant's development with your grandchildren through communication over the telephone, fax, e-mail, etc.

Starting a garden for grandchildren

- ☛ Choose a sunny area of the garden. Make sure it has well-dug soil mixed with manure. This way plants will grow relatively quickly.
- ☛ Visit a nursery and let the grandchildren choose the plants. Steer them to plants that are easy to grow and will take tough treatment. (Children are bound to clamber and squash plants in their enthusiasm.)
- ☛ Forget a harmonious colour co-ordinated garden. Children love bright flowers of assorted colours.
- ☛ Protective barriers such as chicken wire will help a delicate plant to get a good start.
- ☛ Combining flowers, vegetables and herbs provides interest through the seasons.
- ☛ Plants with different textures such as soft velvety leaves to stroke and scented herbs and plants such as lemon verbena are great for adding interest for your grandchildren.
- ☛ Use a combination of fast-sprouting seeds, seedlings and plants in flower so children can see quick-growing results. Children need to see the connection between a seed and the young plant developing later.
- ☛ Choose a mix of perennials and annuals. Perennials add year-round interest while annuals will provide a seasonal splash and interest.

Garden safety

A Grandparent Golden Hint

Replace a dead plant with a similar live one to prevent a young gardener's heartache.

What to plant

Use a combination of seeds and well established seedlings!

Flowers

Grandchildren will love flowers in pots or bunches to take home to keep in their rooms, or as gifts for the family.

- ☛ Nasturtium
- ☛ Forget-me-not
- ☛ Daisies
- ☛ Daffodils
- ☛ Geraniums
- ☛ Marigolds
- ☛ Pansies
- ☛ Snapdragons
- ☛ Sunflowers

Checklist

☑ Have you avoided any plants that could trigger allergies?

☑ Have you taught the children never to eat anything from your garden without asking you whether it is safe?

☑ Have you eliminated sprays that could be harmful to your grandchildren?

☑ Have you taught the children to wash their hands and clean their fingernails and knees. (Dusting their clothes and taking off gardening boots before entering the house keeps your house safe!)

☑ Are you equipped with child-sized tools? They are safer for young hands to use.

Vegetables

One of the best ways to encourage grandchildren to eat fruit and vegetables is to let them pick them straight from the garden.

- ☛ Radishes give fast results. They germinate in about a week and are ready to harvest in six to eight weeks.
- ☛ Carrots provide a great surprise when taken from the soil. Children can also thin out carrots. These are good to eat.
- ☛ Baby tomatoes can be grown in pots and are great to eat as a snack – when they are ripe!
- ☛ Lettuce is another fast-growing vegetable and comes in many different varieties. Loose-hearted lettuces are fun for children because they can be harvested leaf by leaf and eaten in sandwiches, etc.
- ☛ Sweet corn, beans and peas grow quickly and are easily picked.
- ☛ Strawberries and other berries can be grazed as children play in the garden.

Carnivorous Plants!

Use carnivorous plants as the hook to introduce sceptical grandchildren to the fascination of gardening. Observe the plants at work.

Gardening in flats

Large pots or tubs on a balcony are perfect to grow flowering plants or vegetables.

Top quality potting mix, a bit of mixed manure and liquid fertiliser to keep plants looking their best are all that is needed.

Unusual and pretty cacti are great plants for flat dwellers. Caring for them will give grandchildren a sense of achievement – but be careful of the spines. A flat terracotta bowl with a mix of cacti will grow well in a sunny spot in a flat. Select the prettier and more unusual shapes to provide interest.

A young gardener's needs

☞ Hat, gloves and sunblock.
☞ Gumboots in winter, protective shoes in summer
☞ Gardening fork, trowel and spade (Handles painted bright colours will prevent them being lost. Help children to care for tools and return them to a special place for safe keeping until the next visit to the garden).
☞ Small watering can.
☞ Bucket – to carry tools, seedlings, weeds, etc.

Tips for encouraging wildlife to your garden

☞ Grow more plants and trees.
☞ Keep the cat in at night so it doesn't hunt as much.
☞ Have a birdbath and bird-table (away from reach of cats).
☞ Have nest boxes in the garden.

Garden space for grandchildren

It is easy to make your garden a special place for children, a place where children can invent magical worlds and play exciting games.

☛ Interesting playing spaces can be created within your garden at very little cost.

☛ Grandchildren will love hidden spaces where they can create cubby houses and nooks and crannies where they can hide.

☛ Provide some safe garage or shed area where children can put things like chairs and tables and create their own space.

☛ Big cardboard boxes are a short-term option for a cubby. You can keep refrigerator or other appliance boxes in the garage or under the house and drag them into the garden when the children want to play with them.

A digging patch

A digging patch is an 'and/or' alternative for your grandchildren in your garden. Such a patch in the corner of the garden will provide endless hours of enjoyment.

Children can use heavier shovels than those they use in sandpits. And when they add water they get mud – and mud pies! Superb, appetising concoctions can be created.

What a wonderful way to experience nature! Be prepared to grab grandchildren and race them to the bathroom as soon as they tire of playing in the digging patch.

Winter gardening

Winter in the garden is a time for tidying up. Banish the winter blues. Bundle your grandchildren and yourself into coats, collect your gardening gear and escape into the garden. The weather may seem depressing as you look out from inside the house. But once you are working in the garden things will brighten up.

Fishing

Fishing is often regarded as just so much slow action. However, grandparents who are fervent, fishing fanatics know it is a great activity to enjoy with grandchildren.

All you need is a place to fish, reels, rods, fishing tackle and bait and you are set! Dangling a line in water can become a much-loved shared activity. Regular fishing trips can be events that grandparents and grandchildren will enjoy through the years.

For beginner grandparents a little planning and preparation will make the difference between a successful fishing trip with grandchildren and a fishing flop!

Fishing Lore

Encourage fishing ethics and explain them to your grandchildren:

Follow fishing regulations. Release undersize fish to the water unharmed, as soon as possible.

Never take more fish than you need.

Conserve the fishing environment — take away rubbish.

Do not play with fish like toys.

Beginning anglers

Involve grandchildren in the fishing trip from the word go. Give them areas of responsibility such as being in charge of rations.

☛ Take a camera and record catches and great moments from your trip.

☛ Give lots of help and encouragement to young angling grandchildren. Be prepared to assist, and demonstrate over and over and over again basic skills such as tying knots and casting.

☛ Demonstrate how to handle fish with care.

☛ Concentrate on accuracy rather than distance when teaching grandchildren to cast.

Choosing a fishing spot

Select a safe yet practical fishing spot depending on the age and skills of grandchildren. Try to select an area that is easy to reach. Ask among fishing friends for spots that should have suitable fish available.

Estuaries where fresh and salt water tides merge, bays and lakes are all good fishing spots to take grandchildren. Fish tend to be found along or near structures which offer food and protection from bigger fish, such as jetties, rock walls, sunken logs, weed beds and reefs.

Don't fish among a crowd of anglers. Grandchildren have a tendency to get tangled with other anglers when casting!

Fishing safety

- Keep fishing knives sheathed and out of young grandchildren's reach. Keep little fingers away from sharp hooks.
- Take and use plenty of protective sun creams. UV rays reflect from water surfaces.
- Find out if there is any dangerous marine life in the area, for example stone fish.
- Never take chances with the weather. Leave the boat at home if the weather looks dicey.
- Handle fish with care. Most fish have protective spines and you should make your grandchildren aware of this.

Essential equipment

- hats and sunscreen
- rods/reels
- extra tackle
- bait
- food and drink
- correct clothing (be prepared for hot and sunny, cold and wet weather)

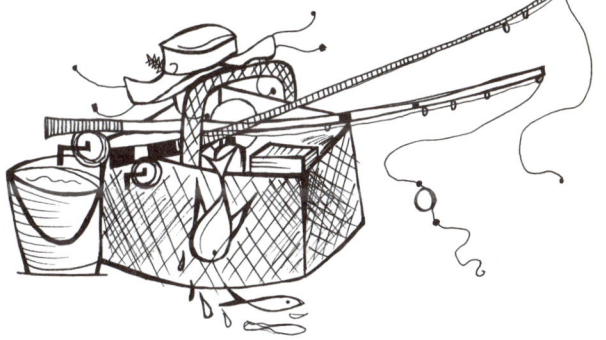

Tackle

Fishing tackle is all the extra bits and pieces that fishing grandparents know are really essential.

For beginner grandparent anglers choose tackle boxes that you and your grandchildren can carry! Don't fill the tackle box with lots of equipment unsuited to the fishing area you have chosen.

Basic fishing tackle could include floats, a few sinkers, lures and a small knife stored in a tray. Small, clear lidded containers for storing hooks, swivels, and sinkers will give safe, easy access.

Casting

Casting keeps grandchildren involved and interested when nibbles are far apart. A double-handed casting method is good for young anglers. Watching the spot they are aiming for is a helpful hint.

Make sure grandchildren are balanced and comfortable when casting. This prevents falls into the water.

Landing a fish

Hooking a fish is only halfway to catching a fish. Landing a fish is what fishing is about. However, to young anglers the actual catch is often not as important as the process of fishing. Don't take over and land your grandchild's fish!

Missing a catch is OK, too, and part of fishing.

Waiting for fish to bite can be a frustrating time for young anglers. Watch the frustration tolerance levels. If they are getting very low, pack up and go while the going is good. Go fishing another time! Remember – forcing kids to go fishing could put them off for life!

Thrills and spills in the snow

Do you crave a well-carved turn? Have you a passion for deep powder? Grandparents who are addicted to the thrills and spills of the ski fields will know there is no reason why grandchildren cannot be introduced to and participate in snow activities.

If you are a grandparent who has also wanted, but never actually had the opportunity, to spend time in snow and ski activities, why not become a new skier and snowboarder with your grandchildren?

A gentle snow experience

Many families take ski holidays. Accept the invitation if you are invited.

You can perform the ultimate in grandparent duties and still have a gentle snow experience. You can supervise young fry between their lessons and other snow activities. Many resorts have children's centres which provide special tow services, lessons and other activities for your grandchildren.

Share your grandchildren's excitement and joy from their experiences in the snow.

Remember, it is not compulsory for grandparents to experience the ultimate ski or snowboarding holiday with all the high adrenaline activity written about in travel articles.

While the family and grandchildren are on the ski fields, find an open fire and nestle down with a good book. Enjoy the snow through a view from the windows.

There is an enormous variety of things to do at snow resorts today and the list gets longer each year. There are snowshoe tours, tobogganing, snowcat tours, movie theatres with latest release films, indoor-heated swimming pools, indoor sports and fully equipped gymnasiums as well as a tremendous variety of restaurants and a lively winter nightlife. And of course there is plenty of material to build a snowman!

Snow travel packages

You don't have to be among the rich and famous enjoying the pizzazz of ritzy ski resorts. There are snow packages to suit all pockets if you want to take your grandchildren to the snow.

Check with travel agents. Many ski resorts offer a range of accommodation. If you decide to take one grandchild or more, weekends in the snow can be affordable and provide exhilarating experiences for everyone.

A day trip to the snowfields can also be exciting and not stretch the pocket or the nerves.

Remember to take masses of clothing to change into, and lots of plastic bags to take home the wet clothing and footwear!

A grandparent's basic guide to the snow

- ☞ Do exercise before your trip such as brisk walking, jogging, cycling and stretching. You don't have to be super fit to enjoy skiing and snowboarding. However, fitter, stronger and more supple people are more likely to avoid injury on the slopes.
- ☞ Choose a resort within easy access. All resorts have specific beginner areas, beginner tickets, beginner packages, lessons and ski/snowboard hire.
- ☞ Check when the snow season starts in various areas. There are always budget-priced packages early in the season when snow can sometimes be marginal. Snowmaking generally ensures that there's enough white stuff for you and your grandchildren to have a great time.
- ☞ Coach travel takes the hassle out of travelling in the snow for grandparents. Remember, if travelling in your own car to resorts you will need anti-freeze in the radiator and to carry chains.

Adventuring in the wild

Grandparents should never fear adventuring in the wild. Visiting the local park can be wild and full of excitement for young grandchildren. (Hint: it is a little more tricky to persuade older grandchildren that real adventures can be found in the local park!)

There are wild places – parks of all kinds – never too far away. Grab a drink and some fruit, take a picnic afternoon tea, packed lunch – go camping – and enjoy the 'wild' outdoors with your grandchildren.

Contact your Government Parks and Gardens Department to locate your nearest open spaces. Select one that matches the age of your grandchildren. You are looking for a 'wild' place where they can explore safely and enjoy being outdoors.

Parks with made paths and tracks, suitable for prams, pushers, trikes and bikes, are ideal for very young grandchildren. Older grandchildren will enjoy unmade paths with plenty of trees and undergrowth to add excitement to their discovering and exploring.

Check out the facilities at the park before you visit. Most 'wild' places provide shelters if the weather turns nasty. Fireplaces and barbecues offer challenging opportunities for outdoor cooking and feasting.

What to look for

☛ Parks with lakes and ponds delight young children. Birds can be fed and closely studied.
☛ Parks with playgrounds are perfect places where the very young can burn up energy.
☛ National parks offer an enormous variety of activities such as bushwalking, picnicking, camping, canoeing, and wildlife watching.
☛ Parks with outdoor cooking facilities provide a challenging change from cooking and dining at home.

Going camping

If you are an experienced, enthusiastic, relaxed camper, definitely go camping with grandchildren. Children adore camping. Sleeping under canvas is magic for them. Camping is a very economical way of holidaying with grandchildren.

However, if you hate the thought of being damp, spending a lot of time crouching and crawling around, being eaten by creepy crawlies, getting dirty or 'roughing it', if you can't survive without the little luxuries of life, don't go camping with grandchildren. Do not even contemplate going camping! It will only lead to disaster and mayhem.

Camping in the garden is a painless option and can be fun for everyone. If worse comes to worst you come inside the house!

Essentials to consider

Planning is essential when going camping. Make lots of lists with grandchildren.

Where to go?

Consider carefully where you will go. Will you go to the mountains, to the beach, a lake or a river, a forest, or your own garden? Will you go to an organised public camp site, to a National Park or a site on private land?

What to take?

Make lots of lists. Tick off items from lists as you collect everything you need.
- ☛ A Shelter List, for example a tent and poles if needed
- ☛ An Equipment List, for example sleeping bags, tables and chairs
- ☛ A Clothing List – individual ones for grandparents and grandchildren
- ☛ An Essentials List, for example towels and biodegradable soap etc.
- ☛ A Cooking List, for example food, utensils etc.
- ☛ An Odds and Ends List, for example medical kit etc.

Warning!

Tell grandchildren not to touch or run fingers along the tent when it is wet. This is sure to start a leak!

The camp site

Arrive early enough in daylight to set up in time for a good night's sleep.

Clear the area before you pitch the tent. Watch out for spiders and ants! Allow space between tents so you can move around freely.

Pitch the tent:
☛ on even ground with a gentle slope so the rain can run off;
☛ in a sheltered area – not in a dry creek bed, under a crumbling rock-face or under a tree;
☛ with the opening cross-wind.

Things to do

What to do should not be a problem when camping with grandchildren. Depending on your site, and the age and interests of you and your grandchildren, you can fish, boat, swim, rock-climb, explore, observe plant and animal life, sketch and paint, write, cloud watch, bushwalk or read in a quiet spot.

At night you can star-gaze, tell ghost stories, read books together, have sing-songs and play board and card games.

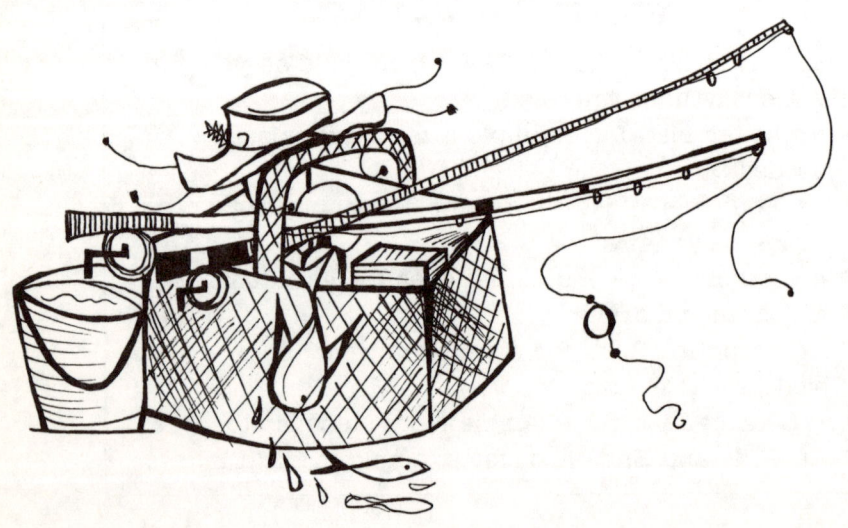

Camp cooking

There is a wide range of outdoor cooking gear available. Be familiar with it before you reach your camping site! Practise cooking a few camp meals at home before setting out in the wild.

☛ Check fire regulations. Open camp fires are banned at many camping sites and especially in certain seasons.

☛ Estimate that grandchildren will eat twice as much when camping as when at home.

☛ Plan meals with grandchildren for each day and buy supplies with care before you set out on the camping trip.

☛ Make sure supplies are kept in secure containers to prevent ants, etc. from invading them.

☛ Be careful with drinking water. Boil river water before drinking it or using it for cooking.

The wilderness code

As visitors to a natural environment we must accept the responsibility to leave it in an undisturbed condition. Here are some wilderness rules:

☛ Carry your rubbish out.

☛ Leave your camp site as you found it. (Only the grass should be flat where the tent stood.)

☛ Guard against all risk of bushfire. If you use a camp fire, return stones to where you found them, scatter the ash, disperse the firewood.

☛ Keep all lakes, rivers and creeks free of polluting agents. Use only biodegradable soap – never detergents.

☛ Human waste should be buried well away from camp sites, water sources and tracks. Toilet paper must be burned.

☛ Leave pets at home.

☛ Keep to made tracks when bushwalking.

Wildlife watching

Grandparents and grandchildren do not need to conquer Mount Everest or discover a new species of dinosaur. All they have to do is walk into the garden or street to discover fascinating and amazing wildlife.

Small animals can be found under logs, rocks, bark or trees. You can discover animals living in a puddle or gutter. You might be lucky and find a frog in a used tyre – lazing in a little water.

In towns and cities you will see possums on rooftops, walking along telephone wires as well as in trees in parks and gardens.

Protect wildlife – and children

- ☞ Tread carefully and watch the ground as you walk. Take care not to destroy small animals' homes. Apart from respecting these animals, some may be dangerous if disturbed, and could bite or sting grandchildren and grandparents.
- ☞ Avoid touching living things with your hands. Do not put your fingers into holes or places you can't see into! If you are not sure what will happen if you pick up a mini-creature, leave it alone.
- ☞ Use a stick to poke about (but cause as little damage as possible), some mini-creatures may be poisonous and could bite or sting. Others may suffer from shock if handled.
- ☞ Do not touch scorpions, spiders, bees, wasps, centipedes or bull-ants.
- ☞ Do not interfere with birds' nests. Touching a bird's nest can result in the parent bird abandoning it altogether.

An Adventurers Code

To observe, explore, enjoy, protect and conserve wildlife and its habitat.

Getting in touch with nature

A Great Adventurers Rule

'Take nothing but photographs and leave nothing but footprints . . . and try not to leave these!'

A nature diary

Keeping a nature diary can give grandchildren a lasting record of their early adventures with you. After adventuring in the outdoors help them to write up their nature diary. Include sketches and records of the dates and times of their observations of plants and animals. Young grandchildren can add drawings to your text. These records will provide fascinating information over time, especially if you keep records of anything unusual or out of place.

Where to explore
- ☞ under bark, rocks and in rotting leaf litter
- ☞ in grass and on leaves
- ☞ in cracks and crevices
- ☞ in water
- ☞ in trees
- ☞ flying free in the air
- ☞ in the ground

Tracks and trails

Look for tracks and trails left by day- and night-time visitors. Follow animal tracks and find out who they belong to. Look in your garden, the street and in the park. Some will be obvious, such as a snail trail or dog tracks in the mud. The sand is a wonderful place to discover patterns of tracks and trails made by sea birds and sea creatures. Become nature detectives, trace and identify more unusual tracks.

Spotlighting

Adventuring outside at night with a spotlight can be great fun and a wonderful opportunity to explore with your grandchildren. You can find possums, owls, spiders, moths and other animals who come out at night for food. The early evening is a great time to watch for birds.

Star gazing

Star gazing is another wonderful activity to do with grandchildren after dark and can open the world of astrology to them.

Identifying plants and animals

Identifying wildlife treasures can be fun research for grandchildren and grandparents. Most people, big and small, like to know the names of things and this includes plants and animals.

Make a research trip to the local library. Invest in a collection of reference books, which cover your particular area, for your own bookshelf. The Internet is also a great place to visit to investigate and discover 'wildlife mysteries' with grandchildren.

'What's this?' is a common question asked by grandchildren. Don't panic if you don't know the answer.

'Let's find out when we go home!' is a great reply. And make sure you do – grandchildren have super memories. If you can't identify the particular insect or bird, grandchildren can think up their own descriptive name. You will be able to identify it one day.

Insect watching

Insect watching is a very satisfying outdoor occupation for grandparents and grandchildren of all ages. There are always plenty of insects around. There are definitely more insects than there are people in the world. Insects live in just about all parts of the world and eat almost anything. In one square metre (one square yard) of your garden there are probably between 500 and 2000 insects.

Grandparents Golden Hint

Remember to take extra clothing for the grandchild who could fall in and the grandparent who has to rescue them!

Nature detectives

Listen and look for insects. Encourage grandchildren to be nature detectives. Watch out for signs such as nibbled leaves etc. Look for:
- ☞ Eggs
- ☞ Cocoons, caterpillars
- ☞ Butterflies and moths
- ☞ Ants, bees
- ☞ Slugs and snails
- ☞ Flies, aphids, ladybirds, grasshoppers, cockroaches, beetles, centipedes and millipedes, bugs, dragonflies and damselflies

Ponding

Ponding is great fun with grandchildren. Aquatic insects are wonderful to observe if you have the opportunity to put them under a microscope. A net to collect aquatic insects is useful equipment.

The opportunity to observe the life cycle of frogs – from egg to tadpole to frog – is another wonderful experience for grandchildren.

Birdwatching

Thousands of grandparents are ardent 'Birdos' or 'Twitchers'! These birdwatching grandparents will know that birdwatching is a tricky pastime to do with young grandchildren. Birdwatchers need to listen carefully and watch quietly. This does not come easily to young grandchildren!

However, watching the behaviour of common birds such as sparrows, starlings, pigeons and seagulls is a great way to introduce grandchildren to the joys of birdwatching.

Enthusiastic young birdwatchers need protective clothing, a note pad and pen, and food and drink when birdwatching in the wild. Binoculars and a bird field book to identify birds add to the fun and interest of discovering different species.

Early morning birdwatching is a great activity to do with early-rising grandchildren. Sit outside with your cup of tea, juice and cereal and watch the birds.

A family of ducks at the park can provide great opportunities for grandchildren to observe how ducklings are taught to feed and when to hide.

Beachcombing and rockpooling

Beachcombing and rockpooling are lovely ambling activities to do with grandchildren. Combing the beach for washed-up treasures such as different shells, seaweed and feathers is great fun.

Different seasons bring different beach treasures to the sand, especially after storms.

Rockpools are fascinating places full of sea-life, such as seaweeds, snails, crabs, sponges and other small sea creatures.

Things to know

Make sure each grandchild wears suitable footwear, hat, and a long-sleeved shirt. A jacket is handy to keep out the wind. Take plenty of sunscreen.

Most rockpool creatures are harmless but a few can be dangerous to humans, such as the blue-ringed octopus.

A seashore safety code

☛ Try not to touch sea animals and remember – rocks are homes for many sea animals. Replace rocks carefully.

☛ Do not remove live sea animals from their environment.

☛ Return collected objects to where you found them.

☛ Watch out for waves.

☛ Read and take notice of signs.

☛ Do not put your hands where you cannot see them.

Caring for the environment

Our grandchildren are well aware of the need to protect and conserve our environment. As we look around our ever-changing world, we become aware that we need to do all we can to help make a safer, healthier planet for our grandchildren.

Grandparents can be positive and provide great role models for grandchildren. Through our example we can guide and support grandchildren in realising that everything we do has an effect on the environment. Everyone can make a difference in sustaining and conserving the environment.

Renewable and non-renewable resources

This is a simple explanation for grandchildren so they can understand the important concept of renewable and non-renewable resources.

Renewable resources are those that can be produced again such as trees. We are able to plant special types of trees to be used as paper.

Non-renewable resources cannot be replaced. The earth has only a limited amount of non-renewable resources. Most non-renewable resources are found deep beneath the Earth's surface. They have to be mined if they are to be used, for instance bauxite ore which is used to make aluminium. We cannot plant more bauxite in the ground and hope it will grow!

Write letters:

if there is an environmental issue that bothers you or your grandchildren;

to report an environmentally friendly activity you have seen;

to pass on an environmental success story.

How to make a difference

Grandparents can demonstrate simple, practical ways to contribute to solving many problems facing our planet. Include grandchildren in activities that you do to refuse, reduce, reuse and recycle waste. Explain how we can use or misuse energy.

Support local action groups and campaigns

As human beings living on this planet we have the right to clean air and water, a safe environment and the natural beauties of this world.

Don't be frightened to let your grandchildren see that you can speak firmly and loudly against people and companies who threaten to take these rights away from us.

Join and/or support community action groups that protect and conserve the local environment. Support campaigns to make people aware of endangered animals and plants and your local environment.

Involve yourself, your grandchildren and families in events such as local Clean Up days and Green Picnics.

Don't be a litterbug!

A simple explanation will help young grandchildren understand the reasons why we shouldn't litter our environment.

Explain to grandchildren that:

☛ littering is ugly;
☛ littering costs money (people have to be paid to pick up litter);
☛ littering pollutes and damages their environment.

Practical things to do

The 4 Rs – Refuse, Reduce, Reuse and Recycle – are important rules to follow to help the environment.

Grandparents can show their grandchildren simple practices that reduce, refuse, reuse and recycle materials such as:

- ☛ Writing on both sides of paper, making scribble pads from recycled paper, etc.
- ☛ Buying drinks in returnable bottles whenever possible
- ☛ Avoiding buying over-packaged goods
- ☛ Buying products made of, or packaged in, recycled material
- ☛ Saving energy by switching off lights, heaters, the TV and radio when they're not being used
- ☛ Wearing an extra layer of warm clothing rather than turning on the heater
- ☛ Not dropping litter
- ☛ Passing clothes, old toys, books and games on to someone else or giving them to charity shops
- ☛ Using collections or banks for cans, waste paper and bottles
- ☛ Making sure food scraps are composted
- ☛ Saving energy and reducing pollution by walking, cycling and using public transport whenever possible
- ☛ Using water wisely; help grandchildren to understand water is our most precious resource.

Begin with small changes!

If you haven't been into refusing, reducing, reusing or recycling before, it's a good idea to start with only the things you feel comfortable doing.

As you become used to some of the smaller changes, it will be easier to move on to bigger changes.

It is important to keep our natural environment in good condition so you and your children's children and their children and children's children can enjoy them!

Food chains and food webs

Sometimes grandchildren can become upset by the apparent violence of nature. This is a simple explanation for young grandchildren so they can understand food chains and food webs and how all living things live together and are linked in the environment.

Explain that:

☞ a plant uses the sun's energy to grow: a plant-eating animal (a herbivore) eats the plant;

☞ meat-eating animal (a carnivore) or a plant- and meat-eating animal (an omnivore) then eats the herbivore – this series of events is called a food chain;

☞ a food web is several food chains linked together in an ecosystem.

Draw diagrams

Use diagrams and arrows to explain this concept to young grandchildren!

Remember:

☞ a young tadpole eating water weeds is a herbivore;

☞ a small fish feeding on whatever it can find, water weeds to tiny animals such as a tadpole, is an omnivore;

☞ an adult frog catching and eating small animals such as flies is a carnivore.

Travelling with grandchildren

Travelling with grandchildren can be problematic to say the least. However, harmonious travelling with grandchildren is a possibility. One to be attained!

Travelling age groups

Travelling grandchildren can often be divided into roughly four age groups: babies, toddlers, older children and teenagers. Be honest. If you are not comfortable with particular age groups or you don't feel energetic enough to last a long-haul journey, don't go. Travelling with families and grandchildren is a full-on occupation.

Babies

Babies need a lot of equipment. They like routine for naps, feeding and changing. Some babies may get very anxious if they are on the move. However, babies are very portable and some are very easy to entertain.

Toddlers

Toddlers can be difficult at the best of times, even on their home base. They have a never-ending supply of energy and are always on the go. Holidaying with toddlers means you need to keep constant watch over them in different surroundings.

Older children

Travelling with older children from five years on, can be a real pleasure but still hard work. If you are considering a holiday with older grandchildren you will need to plan co-operatively and make an effort to include their likes and dislikes.

Teenagers

Teenagers can be a group on their own. Will they share your love of museums and art galleries, mountain trekking or fishing? Are you happy to spend days with your teenage grandchildren, doing their thing? Are you prepared for the responsibility of taking them on a holiday with you? And more importantly, do you have the physical fitness to cope with emergencies if they arise?

Aircraft travel

Travelling on an aircraft can take a long, long time . . . especially when you consider international flights. Combine this with the average concentration span of a small grandchild and you could be in big trouble.

Travelling on aircraft can be difficult for grandparents at the best of times. Travelling with grandchildren on aircraft can be a frightening experience. However, with a little planning it can become a survivable experience.

When flying, don't always rely on airline travel packs for children. Bring your own extra activities to supplement them.

What to take

- ☛ Allow young grandchildren to bring a favourite toy. A small favourite toy! Remember cabin luggage should be kept to a minimum and you have to carry it.
- ☛ Let children wear their most comfortable clothes. Bring a change of clothing.
- ☛ Take advantage of children's meals on airlines.
- ☛ Pack some extra drinks. Flying is very dehydrating. Make sure children drink plenty of fluids.
- ☛ Pack a few snacks – treats you know grandchildren will enjoy.
- ☛ Take several different activities for children to try, especially during long trips. Young children tire quickly of the one activity. Introducing something new for the flight – books or 'small' toys – is a help too.
- ☛ Pushers, strollers and baby car seats should be checked in with your baggage.
- ☛ For older children sucking lollies for take-off and landing can help when their ears are affected.

Flying tips for grandparents – (not on a broomstick!)

☞ Drink plenty of water – frequently walk to the aircraft water fountain.

☞ Try to sleep on long sections of the flight. Wear eye masks, close blinds, ask for a pillow or bring your own.

☞ Walk around the aircraft regularly during the flight. Do exercises in a seated position to stretch muscles in legs, feet, arms and neck.

Going by car

Travelling by car is easier than travel by air. You can stop whenever you feel like it. Find a playground. Children can run around and let off steam.

Car travel tips

☞ Grandchildren should wear comfortable clothes and have spares.

☞ You will need plenty of non-messy food and drinks in resealable containers.

☞ Chill water for cool sips along the road.

☞ Make sure small grandchildren in car seats have a good view.

☞ Prepare and take a travelling survival kit of bits and pieces to entertain and pass the time.

☞ Bring some cassettes of favourite songs.

☞ Sing songs and play games such as 'Spotto' and 'I spy'.

☞ Stop frequently to give children a chance to stretch their legs.

Train travel

Travelling by train is a great option for grandparents and grandchildren. There is room to move about, sit, read or play 'quiet' games.

You may even get a good night's sleep if you are travelling on a long-distance train with sleeping compartments.

A train travel survival kit

Individual travel survival kits for grandchildren can keep them occupied during a long haul. Include activities with different levels of difficulty depending on the age of children.

Include:
- Finger puppets
- Cards
- Stickers
- Activity books and puzzles
- Pens, coloured pencils and sharpeners
- Dice and lap-sized board games

Travel ideas for young children

- A lidded cup with a spout
- Teaspoon – handy when you are only given a knife and fork
- A plastic bowl to use when you share a meal or put together a meal from yours
- A large bag to carry disposable nappies (can be used to carry purchases as the nappies are used)
- A mop-up cloth, bibs, wet wipes and other cleaning material
- A travelling electric element for boiling water – a help in the preparation of simple meals such as noodles
- A familiar fluffy toy for bedtime
- A few favourite toys, books, pencils and paper
- Two armchairs facing each other can make a fine safe sleeping cot for a small child
- A large drawer can also serve as a cot for a baby

Eating out

When travelling with grandchildren:

- Choose restaurants that are not crowded. If you eat early you may miss the crowds. Restaurants where you can eat outside are also worth looking for.
- Check the menu to make sure there is something grandchildren can eat.
- Entrees are often the right amount of food for children. Sharing a meal can work out too.

Travelling alone with children

Make sure grandchildren are prepared for travelling experiences. Get plenty of practice at eating in restaurants. Go for trips. Get in lots of walking practice. Read about and research the places you are going to with grandchildren. Watching movies and videos creates anticipation.

☞ Decide sightseeing musts in advance. Don't overdo the travel guides. One is plenty for a reference.

☞ Keep grandchildren informed of your plans and what will be happening every day.

☞ Value grandchildren's experiences. Don't always turn their attention to what you feel is a more important aspect of what they see.

☞ Leave some unstructured time each day for play or mooching.

☞ Make sure you arrive at your destination early in the afternoon to explore and settle in.

☞ Be fussy with hotel rooms. (You can be assertive and friendly.) Check to see your room first. If it has been arranged previously by a travel agent do not take your luggage straight to your room. You will have more bargaining power if you are holding up a queue in the hotel lobby.

☞ Be strong. Do not relent and allow grandchildren access to the mini-bar. The hotel bill can blast sky high if numerous chocolate bars and bottles of mineral water are consumed. Set rules for grandchildren making telephone calls through hotel switchboards and when using pay TV.

Number plate games

☞ Keep a list of number plates that make words.
☞ Look for number plates that can be rearranged to make words.
☞ Make messages out of the letters, for example; WFD 567 could be 'What's for dinner?'

'I spy with my little eye . . .'

'I spy' is an old favourite and one of the best travel games.

One player chooses an object and says, 'I spy with my little eye something beginning with A.'

The player who guesses the correct answer chooses the next object.

Limit the game to objects found inside the car or train carriage.

'Spotto' games

'Spotto' games work beautifully. Grandchildren need to sit quietly and observe different things.

For example:

☞ Spot the yellow cars, brown cows, police stations, telephone boxes, clock towers. Various objects can equal different scores.
☞ The player first to spot an object scores. Highest scores win.
☞ Spot specific colours or kinds of cars, for instance – a red Ferrari!
☞ Spot the foreign number plates – interstate and overseas. The player who first spots an interstate number plate scores 1 point, an overseas number plate scores 3 points.
☞ The player with the highest score wins.

Holidays

Grandparents usually have plenty of time for holidays. So be flexible! Be prepared to pack and 'take-off' with the family or even alone with grandchildren. Careful planning is needed when grandchildren spend school holidays with you. Watch out for and avoid possible pitfalls that can happen during holidays that involve grandchildren.

Family holidays

Grandparents are often invited on family holidays. These holidays should be a chance to unwind, have fun and spend time together in a relaxed atmosphere. Unfortunately, sometimes the longed-for break can turn into a survival exercise.

Think carefully before you accept invitations for a family holiday.

An extended period of time with grandchildren is not every grandparent's idea of a perfect holiday. No matter how much you love them, some hard-to-handle grandchildren can be very difficult to live with day-in and day-out.

Be prepared. Babies and toddlers need constant parenting routines. Older grandchildren look to be entertained and demand great hunks of time.

Tensions can flare among children of varying ages and temperaments, and remember you will not be the final decision-maker.

However, be that as it may, staying home or limiting travel to the safest, easiest options could deny you a fantastic experience and happy, lifelong memories for you and your grandchildren.

A Grandparent Golden Hint

A combination of refreshed parents and grandparents equals more fun for children.

Handy tips for family holidays

Grandparents can suggest some of these strategies . . . tactfully!

- ☛ Share chores. Have rosters. Everyone can be given chores and be expected to do them. Children can work in teams with adults.
- ☛ Allocating a set amount of pocket money before the holiday begins can stop constant requests for ice creams, mini-golf, etc.
- ☛ Make times for adults to have relaxing activities. (Parents and grandparents can share supervision responsibilities and take turns to do their own thing – play golf, a snooze by the pool, etc.)
- ☛ Selecting a holiday place where there will be other children for companionship can be a lifesaver. Resorts that cater for children, camping and caravan holidays are great places where grandchildren can make new friends.
- ☛ If you are staying in an up-market place with little rooms or bungalows around or near the dining and entertainment area, adults can take turns to go back to the rooms to check if children are still sleeping.
- ☛ Holidaying with young children can mean days start early and usually end early. Adults – this includes grandparents – can work in shifts and give each other a break to do their own thing.
- ☛ If you are feeling a bit martyrish, don't hesitate . . . take a day off. Better a contented, happy travelling grandparent than a miserable one. Why not suggest that parents take a day off too? You will hold the fort!
- ☛ Caution: watch grandchildren like hawks at stations, airports, etc. Parents and grandparents are often distracted with finding taxis, making new connections, and so on.

School holidays

School Holidays are when grandparents are absolutely indispensable. Grandparents come into their own as 'Fill the Gap' specialists.

A little planning and organisation will help you sail through school holidays with a smile on your face and low blood pressure.

Outdoor things to do

Finding and doing 'outdoor things' is absolutely essential during school holidays when grandchildren are in your care.

- ☞ Check with friends.
- ☞ Ring around your local area.
- ☞ Watch, read and listen to the media for information on available activities.
- ☞ Visit and check out local facilities, for example library, park, swimming pool.
- ☞ Find out the times when facilities are available. Are special activities provided during holiday times? Do you have to book?
- ☞ List dates, opening times, place and age-level suitability of facilities or activities.
- ☞ Draw up an Action Plan.
- ☞ Plan what you will do.
- ☞ Book early!

Holidaying with the grandchildren

Choosing the right accommodation is three-quarters of the way to a happy holiday for you and your grandchildren. Don't go overboard. Make sure it is within your budget.

The beach

Depending on the grandchildren, you will need safe conditions for toddlers and a few waves for older children and teenage body-boarders.

Resorts with kids' clubs

These are the holiday equivalent to daycare centres – qualified child care workers take the grandchildren off your hands for at least a few hours every day. (A good chance of a rest here for grandparents!) Often such clubs are free and included with packaged resort prices.

Hotels

Hotels are often ill-equipped to deal with families. See that you are not crammed into one room with roll-away beds and cots. However, two rooms often fail to provide access through an adjoining door. Then a family room is the best option.

Apartments

Apartments are a better choice than hotels when you are staying in the city with children. You have room to move and can cut the costs by shopping at supermarkets and cooking your own meals.

Holiday houses

Holiday houses are a great choice. It is best if you can view them before the holiday. Again you will have room to move, not only inside, but there will probably be an outside area suitable for play and relaxation. Cooking your own meals is a great cost saver.

Or . . . how about a cruise?

Cruises

Cruising with grandchildren? Why not? Today cruising can be affordable and fun. There are a number of cruise lines that operate packages especially targeted to the family – and grandparent – market.

Cruise packages that cater for grandchildren offer extensive activity programs to keep grandchildren happy. They can make crafts, watch videos and play games while parents and grandparents are relaxing on the top deck.

A Grandparent Golden Hint

A rest helps keep everyone on an even keel.

Tips for cruising grandparents

☛ Take a short cruise of two or three days to test your sea going legs. (Who wants to be sea-sick for the entire cruise?)

☛ Think carefully if you are considering being part of a family deal, such as having a bunk in a cabin with two, three or more grandchildren. Will you last the distance without losing your cool? Will your late-night entrances disturb the grandchildren?

☛ Book a waterline room – best for children and grandparents inclined to motion sickness.

☛ Make sure children's programs are offered all the year. Some cruise lines offer their children's programs only if there are enough children booked on the cruise.

☛ Check the ages required for children to be included in the activities, the activities offered and the ratio of support staff to children.

☛ Happy Cruising!

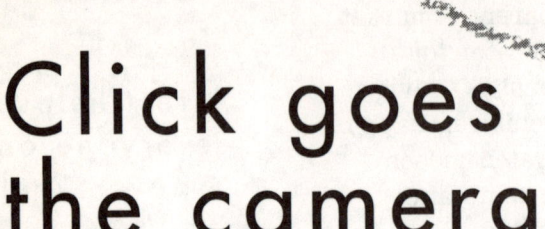

Click goes the camera

Grandparents, grandchildren and cameras go together. Invest in a camera and get clicking! Waiting for friends and family to take treasured shots of grandchildren is too frustrating!

A beginner's guide

So you want to become a 'shutterbug'? Cameras and films are so good today it is not hard to take a successful photo. Some cameras are simple to work, some are more complicated. Only the buttons and dials on cameras change.

When buying a camera look for one that is quick and easy to use and feels good in your hands. The automatic point-and-shoot cameras, either with a 35 mm fixed lens, or preferably with a zoom and built-in flash, are an excellent buy. As you become more competent you can invest in more expensive cameras.

Films and processing

Films will take either 12, 24, or 36 shots. Have several films on hand which have fewer shots, then you can have one processed at a time. This will give you time to evaluate your photographic skills and ask yourself some questions. Are you overdoing it, for example taking more shots of one grandchild than another?

Watch out for special processing deals that enable you to have multiple copies processed cheaply or selected photographs enlarged. The photo lab will help you select photographs that will enlarge successfully. Look for sharp and clear photographs. Remember enlargements cost more than regular-size pictures.

Hold it!

Hold still while you press the shutter button! Press gently. Don't push so hard that you jiggle the camera. If you do you will get a blurry picture/shot.

Taking the photo

Hold the camera still and straight! Rest the camera on something if you are a bit shaky. Make sure your finger, hair or the strap of the camera doesn't block the lens. Explore different ways of using your camera. You can turn the camera so your picture is vertical or diagonal rather than horizontal.

Take steps!

Step forward or back, or move to one side, until you see exactly what you want in your shot.

Your subjects – darling grandchildren – should fill half the space in your viewfinder, otherwise they will be hard to see in your photograph.

The most common mistake amateur photographers can make is not getting close enough to the subject, for example the grandchildren. Take four steps closer. If you find you are then too close, take two big steps back (mind you don't fall over!). If you are too close your photo will be blurry.

Using your viewfinder

What you see inside the 'frame' of your viewfinder will be your photo!

- ☞ Frame your shots carefully.
- ☞ Mind you don't cut off your grandchild's head or feet. Put the grandchildren in the middle of the frame.
- ☞ Try to look at things differently. You can shoot a 'bird's-eye view' by standing on something high and shooting down. You can shoot a 'worm's-eye view' by lying on the ground and shooting up at something. Again, watch you don't injure yourself in your photographic enthusiasm!
- ☞ Place your grandchildren – gently – in front of a simple background. This makes for a better shot. First check out suitable backgrounds around your home or theirs. This prevents the 'boredom' aspect of grandchildren being photographed yet again by Grandma or Grandpa.

Indoor photography

You can take good photographs indoors. Use any patch of sunlight coming into the room from a window or open door. Turn on the lights in the room. Check out interesting backgrounds.

You can take photographs indoors from a window. If it is sunny and bright outside, press the camera lens right against the window. The lens must touch the glass or you might see its reflection, along with the grandchildren. Hold your camera still.

Handy camera hints

☛ Don't touch the lens with your fingers. Keep it clean with a clean cotton cloth.
☛ Check the film container for the number of shots available. Never try to open the cartridge or the film will be ruined.
☛ Never leave your camera in direct sunlight or in a closed car in the sun.
☛ If you invest in a tripod you will be able to take a photo of the grandchildren and you!

Landscapes or cityscapes

Landscapes or cityscapes make great travel photographs. Look for patterns and lines. It could be a row of buildings against the skyline, or a group of shells on the sand. Lines convey a sense of distance and depth. Winding roads, tree lines and fences can be used to draw the eye toward your grandchild. If grandchildren accompany you on your travels your photos will be proof of having been there.

Use the rule of two-thirds. Instead of placing your horizon through the centre of the frame, give the land or the sky two-thirds.

Sharing photographs

Sharing photographs of grandchildren is a popular and essential pastime for grandparents. Viewing is usually compulsory for trapped friends, relatives or reciprocal for friends who also have grandchildren.

You will find you need plenty of copies of photos. Copies for your Grandma or Grandpa mini-album, handbag or wallets, plus copies for families. Framed photographs are always necessary for your home. They also make great presents for families. Mailing photographs of grandchildren to absent grandparents is always appreciated.

Do not end up with drawers crammed full of envelopes filled with photographs. Label them with relevant information, that is the names of grandchildren, date, and where the photo was taken. Keep photos in order of some kind. Grandparents are often called on to have a copy of Freddie or Annie for 'My Life' school projects.

Photo albums

A good way to share and show off your photographs is to keep them in an album. Grandchildren just adore looking at photos of themselves.

You can make albums for yourself. Keep one for each year. Or you can make them for the family or for grandchildren and keep them at your home. The latter is a great idea for separated families. Possessions are hard to keep track of when they are spread between two homes.

Keep photos as memories of the happy times you spend with your grandchild. Soon they will be able to take their own photographs. 'This is Your Life' albums can make invaluable life-long treasures for grandchildren.

Travel photography

- Buy postcards instead of photographing icons, for example the Eiffel Tower.
- Concentrate on taking pictures that interest you, then you can add your own personal style.
- Think about taking a throwaway camera on your trip. They are great to use when you don't want to risk your own camera.
- Underwater cameras are useful if you're going to the beach, fishing, sailing or anywhere that could be wet.
- See if your camera equipment and film can be inspected by hand rather than X-rayed when you go through customs.
- Make sure you know where your exposed film is and have it well packed. It is irreplaceable.
- Make sure your camera is packed well and protected from dust and sun. Disguise expensive looking camera bags and equipment. Put your camera inside a simple travel bag.
- Don't take what you can't carry. Consider using a small backpack for camera equipment.
- A small bag around your waist is ideal for carrying a compact camera.
- Have a spare roll of film in your pocket.
- Test all cameras and lenses, especially new ones, before you leave.

Useful gift

Throwaway cameras are useful gifts for grandchildren.

They are great to take on holidays or on school camps etc.

Happy, healthy grandparents

No matter how devoted you are, you must take care of yourself so grandchildren get the best deal.

If you are healthy and happy around your grandchildren, they will feel relaxed and secure.

Watch your own health and stress levels. Make sure you have time to relax.

Only do activities with your grandchildren when you are relaxed and will enjoy them.

If you are writing a blockbuster novel – and have been waiting all your life to do it – you will not want your grandchildren anywhere near you, or your computer or pen, when you are writing.

If you are a grandparent with a busy career, spending time with the grandchildren will slow you down and help you rediscover the little pleasures in life.

Calming techniques

Avoid bottling up stress. This could lead to an explosion that could be harmful and frightening for grandchildren.

☛ Go for a walk.
☛ Do yoga.
☛ Talk to understanding friends.

Caring for grandchildren, whether on a temporary or permanent basis, needs careful management so you can operate at your best.

Watch that you don't over-commit yourself and become irritable and exhausted. Don't run your fuel tank on empty.

Sports to try

Body building, tae kwon-do, tai-chi, yoga, archery, cycling, swimming, pool, lawn bowls, ten-pin bowling, cricket, orienteering, figure skating, croquet, tennis, golf, bushwalking, white water canoeing, snorkelling, aerobics, water aerobics . . . even triathlons, decathlons and other marathon events.

Looking after yourself

Grandparents are usually so busy looking after everyone else they forget to look after themselves. However, remember that if you break down, replacements and spare parts are hard to find!

'Looking after yourself' varies from situation to situation for grandparents. There is 'looking after yourself' when grandchildren are in your care, and there is 'really looking after yourself', the kind you should do in your everyday life.

When grandchildren are in your care

- Make sure you make a meal for yourself when making meals for the grandchildren
- Take a few minutes to telephone a friend or the family. Speaking with an adult will give you a boost!
- Whenever you get a chance – for instance by some miracle the grandchildren might have all co-ordinated their nap time – sit down with a cup of tea and listen to your favourite music.
- Make sure you get out of the house everyday, for example going for a walk with grandchildren.
- If you are looking after grandchildren on a long-term live-in basis, arrange with a friend or neighbour to babysit so you can go out or have a rest.
- Have your favourite music playing around the house.
- Plan your day or week efficiently. Make a list for each day in order of priority. When you have a list of all that is required it is easier to organise your time and jog your memory.
- When doing 'in-house' grandparent duty – for example due to arrival of a new baby or sickness of a parent – keep a temporary calendar large enough to note the grandchildren's activities. Teenage grandchildren can be responsible for writing their own commitments on the calendar.
- Plan and freeze food ahead for long-term visits. Every time you cook casseroles or bake, double, treble or quadruple the quantities to be used for family visits. Make sure you add the date of freezing on packaging!
- Plan and prepare activities before grandchildren's visits, for example make playdough, organise a collage or painting. Prepare them the night before if grandchildren are on a short-term visit.
- For long-term visits keep your visiting, shopping and doctor's appointments, etc together for an 'Expedition Day'.

Really 'looking after yourself'

☞ Ask for support when you need it.

☞ Be realistic and keep positive.

☞ Take time out to relax from the clatter of daily life.

☞ Keep learning from everything you do without judging yourself.

☞ Do not waste time on trivia.

☞ Always know what you want so others cannot tell you.

☞ Do something new . . . enrol in a short course to get the brain ticking again, journey to places unknown; learn a new activity; buy something for yourself that you would not buy before.

☞ Take time to look at the beauty around you.

☞ Treat yourself to a massage, perm, facial, groovy haircut!

☞ Take responsibility for your body. If your medical needs are not being met by your doctor, find a better one.

☞ Smile and laugh . . . be cheerful, enjoy life.

☞ Be in control of your own finances.

☞ Stop saving things for 'best'. Enjoy that aftershave or perfume! Use the best china. Wear your best clothes.

☞ Do something for others . . . become a volunteer, for example Meals on Wheels.

☞ Make sure you are eating a balanced diet.

Forget the saying 'If a job is worth doing it's worth doing well! When grandchildren are around, any 'mop up' is better than no 'mop up' at all.'

Getting older

Getting older is an indisputable fact for everyone on this planet. Every day we live we get a little older. The thing is to be positive and not to dwell on yourself or let it interfere in relationships with your grandchildren, family and friends.

Maintaining good health means, for all of us, making sure our diet and exercise plan are working so we can still enjoy the good things in life.

Good Health

Sharing activities with young grandchildren is one of the great joys of life. We need to look for a realistic way of maintaining fitness and health in order to enjoy our grandchildren.

It is important to keep our mobility and muscular strength. Our bodies as well as our minds, need to be flexible and adaptable. The term 'well-being' differs from grandparent to grandparent. For some it means being adventurous and outgoing, for others, calm and relaxed.

All grandparents need to be alert and focused when they are responsible for grandchildren.

A positive attitude

☛ Maintaining a positive attitude to life is essential for grandparents. To be comfortable and happy with yourself is vital.

☛ Grandparents do not need to 'act their age'! They do not need to settle for a sedentary life!

☛ Enjoy the past . . . as we keep growing so does our past.

☛ Focus on the present . . . forget the 'If onlys'.

☛ It's never too late to begin a new interest. Try a little singing, dancing, surfing, rock-climbing, riding a bike or a motorbike. Take that gentle – or vigorous – walk in the park or along a beach.

Variety in exercise

There is an enormous variety of exercise and sporting activities available to suit all ages, tastes and levels of fitness.

If you don't like exercising alone, join a group! Set your grandchildren a good example. Avoid being fitness challenged! Don't be a couch potato!

Remember you're not aiming for sporting greatness. You are just looking for a physical activity that will – in time – keep you fit.

Stretching

Stretching is a very underrated form of exercise. Stretching irons out the 'creases in your muscles' and minimises the risk of injury.

Injuries can happen at any time, with a given or sudden exertion or change of direction occurring in the simplest of activities, such as catching a ball thrown by an enthusiastic grandchild.

Stretching increases your flexibility or range of motion. This is most important for 'age-challenged' humans. Stretching should be the warm-up and cool-down of any physical activity. It prepares your body for the stresses associated with the exercise to follow.

Developing a routine of simple stretches which you can perform every day maintains flexibility and prevents the muscles from tightening up. Repeating different stretches throughout the day, especially after sitting in the car or doing some other sedentary activity, helps loosen up the body again and keeps aches and pains at bay.

There are stretches you can do for all parts of the body . . . the hands, back, neck and shoulders, legs, feet, head and face.

Caution: if you are unaccustomed to exercise, start slowly. Progress gradually. Refer to experts before you begin on a daily exercise plan.

A Grandparents Golden Rule!

Move it or lose it!

Walking

Exercise need not mean pumping weights at a gym or swimming fifty laps, although many grandparents perform the latter exercises brilliantly.

Walking is a simple and an excellent form of exercise for all ages. Walking lifts the spirits, improves your health, and saves money on parking fees and petrol.

You can walk alone, with your grandchildren, with your dog, with a friend, or you can join a walking club. Walking helps weight loss, reduces blood pressure as well as having other health benefits. It is a great way to 'tune-up' the body.

If you can chat with a grandchild without puffing, while walking, you are doing well.

A Grandparent Golden Rule!

Don't overdo it!

Walking tips

☛ Wear comfortable walking shoes with a support arch and heel.
☛ Wear socks with a stitched heel to prevent their slipping when you are walking.
☛ Don't forget a hat for protection from the sun.

Walking technique

☛ Choose a natural, comfortable stride length, appropriate to your body size, that is no giant striding if you are a vertically challenged grandparent!
☛ Swing your arms in rhythm with your body.
☛ Make sure your body is comfortably upright – no need to be ramrod straight.
☛ Keep your shoulders back but relaxed.
☛ Look straight ahead and lean forward slightly.
☛ Breathe freely and normally.

Returning home

When you return home from a stay with the family or when grandchildren have returned after staying in your home, there is a period of readjustment needed. It is good to know this and to be prepared for it.

When the grandchildren go

The grandchildren's stay with you has been too good to be true! Everything has been perfect! Weather beautiful. No damaged or lost grandchildren. Everyone has been healthy and have got on famously with each other.

It's been a dream of a stay . . . except till now. On the very last day all hell has broken loose. Grandchildren are fighting and complaining. You feel miserable, lonely and rejected. Chaos reigns supreme!

Don't worry. This is the 'we're getting ready to go home tomorrow' syndrome – the going-home transition.

What has happened is that you have all been having a very good time. Grandchildren now need to let go of your care and routine, and begin looking forward to returning home.

☛ Recognise that the visit is over. Encourage grandchildren to share their feelings with you.

☛ Tell them you understand they're looking forward to returning to their family. Let your grandchildren know how much you will miss them and the special times you have shared together. Talk about future visits.

☛ Take your grandchildren's last day with you slowly. Help them to pack and prepare for the trip home. Making or buying small gifts to take home to family members can be part of the last day.

☛ Make sure there is plenty of time for relaxed unpacking at the other end of their journey. They need to get a good night's sleep so they can make a smooth re-entry into their everyday lives.

Grandparents returning home

Grandparents can feel equally horrible – irritable – sad – when they come to the end of a pleasant stay in the family's home.

Allow yourself ample time for packing, and for an unhurried and peaceful journey, whether you're driving or travelling some other way.

Give yourself plenty of time to settle in at home with ease – in the daylight hours.

Now you are on your own . . .

When the grandchildren have finally left, when you have said your last farewell, blown the last goodbye kiss, the silence can seem deafening. Now is the time to enjoy the peace.

☛ Luxuriate in the simple things of life! The long uninterrupted telephone calls to your friends, listening to your favourite radio programs, watching your favourite TV programs, reading the newspaper. Getting back to that block-buster book.

☛ Instead of bedlam, enjoy the tranquillity. Grab hold of that inner calm again. Loiter, linger, dawdle. Have quiet cups of tea, cook your favourite food. Spend time gazing out of windows, contemplating cobwebs in the garden.

☛ Recognise that the visit is over. You will miss the grandchildren's kisses and cuddles, their winning smiles as well as their irresistible capacity for adventure and fun.

☛ Don't be sad. Rejoice! Enjoy the peace. Be content!

Remember you are not an unnatural grandparent . . . you are just rejoicing and luxuriating in the peace and the calm which comes infrequently, but can come, and is the due of all grandparents.

Tomorrow start thinking about climbing those mountains or enrolling in bagpipe lessons!

Part 2:
Things to do

Time-tested activities

Sometimes it is enough to have just one or two activities on hand for your grandchildren to do. Other days you will wish you'd prepared a hundred. It's even a good idea to take materials for an activity or two when you visit grandchildren.

Activities can be as simple as painting and drawing, papier mâché or making puppets.

Plan to do the activities in the morning when grandchildren, and grandparents, have plenty of energy. There is a theory that once you have 'connected' with a young grandchild in the morning, they will demand less of your time for the rest of the day. This is a comforting thought, so keep the afternoon for quieter, more relaxing things to do.

In the following pages are some time-tested activities. Many will bring back memories of your childhood. Some will work better for you and your grandchildren than others. Once started you will quickly be able to add more workable activities to your list.

Being prepared

If you know that your grandchildren are going to spend time with you, either just flying visits, or to stay, it is useful to have a variety of materials 'at the ready'. An easy-to-clean space where children can feel free to play is also important.

An odds-and-ends box

Keep an odds-and-ends box. Collect all those things like buttons, shells, nuts and seed boxes, old birthday cards, scraps of materials and keep them together. This box will be a treasure trove when grandchildren are looking for material to make things.

Art and craft supplies

It pays dividends to always have some art and craft supplies on hand. These should include child-proof scissors, glue, tape, a collection of good quality pens, coloured pencils and felt-tip pens as well as paper, drawing pads and old magazines.

An activity area

Designate an area where your grandchildren will be able to draw, cut and paste. Choose somewhere convenient near water . . . maybe your kitchen. It is a wise grandparent who invests in two or three plastic shower curtains or plastic sheeting for protection of tables and/or bench tops and the areas under and around tables.

Cleaning up

Always include grandchildren in cleaning up. Help them to get started. Set a time limit. Offer a pleasant reward such as 'When we have cleaned up we'll go to the park!' to encourage children to finish the task quickly.

Display

Make sure you have an area in your home where grandchildren's artwork can be displayed. The children will feel their work is valued and appreciated.

Why not have one or two of your grandchildren's masterpieces laminated or framed to go on your walls? Framed artwork can be changed as children produce different creations!

Handy Hint

When very young grandchildren have finished an activity and have created an absolute disaster area, sit them close by. Talk to them while you clean up quickly and efficiently!

The Grandparents Rule of Flexibility

Remember, you have the right to cancel at any time, anywhere, any organised activity in order to enjoy 'mooching' or 'mucking about' with your grandchildren.

Compile a list

Your list should include things to do when grandchildren come visiting, or when you visit them. In order to survive well, 'things to do' need to be separated into two groups – 'things to do indoors' and 'things to do outdoors'.

Most times you won't need to do anything special or planned with your grandchildren. You just need to tuck them under your wing and include them in your daily activities. You can also include them when you are 'mooching' and 'mucking about'.

Other times you will be desperate to find something to do. These are the times when it is wonderful to have a list of 'things to do' close at hand.

Mooching and mucking about

Grandparents are highly skilled in these creative doings. Many children are locked into programs of after-school activities and tight schedules. Mooching and mucking about could be all they want to do when they are with you.

Consider:
- ☞ Relaxing
- ☞ Talking
- ☞ Listening
- ☞ Reading books
- ☞ Going for little walks
- ☞ Cooking some nice food
- ☞ Contemplating a spider's web
- ☞ Doing a little weeding, etc. etc. etc. etc.

Puppets

Puppets are magic and guaranteed to fascinate grandchildren of all ages.

Puppets come in all shapes and sizes. Their complexity can be increased according to the age of your grandchildren. For very young grandchildren you will need to help, if not make the puppets yourself.

Puppets provide lots of fun when they are used in impromptu plays and performances.

Making puppets

There are many different types of puppets and you will see from the instructions below that they are relatively easy to make.

Sock puppets

You will need:
- socks
- assorted materials such as felt, ribbon, wool and fabric scraps, buttons, feathers, sequins
- glue
- needles
- wool

What to do:
- ☛ Discuss with your grandchildren how you are going to make puppets.
- ☛ Talk about whether the puppet is going to have eyes. How you are going to make the eyes? (Buttons, sewn on very securely, are excellent for eyes.)
- ☛ Is the puppet going to have a mouth? Does it need a mouth? Can a mouth be made by moving fingers inside the sock?
- ☛ Allow children to select their own materials to create an animal, person or 'thing' puppet. The sky is the limit!
- ☛ Children can sew and/or glue materials to make their puppet.
- ☛ Enjoy performing! Let your hair go!
- ☛ Send puppets home with grandchild or store puppets at your house for a rainy day!

Puppet Golden Hints

A hand inserted into the sock will prevent sewing or gluing both sides of the sock together.

Use darning needles with big eyes to make threading easy!

Wooden-spoon puppets

You will need:

- a wooden spoon
- felt-tip pens
- wool for hair
- crepe paper, scraps of material, aluminium foil
- glue

What to do:

☞ Paint a face on the wooden spoon.

☞ Glue wool on for hair or fur.

☞ Use crepe paper, material or foil to wrap around the handle to serve as clothes.

Hand puppets

You will need:

- fabric
- thread
- needles
- scissors
- felt-tip pen or marker
- glue
- buttons, wool and scraps of material

What to do:

☞ Grandchildren place their hand – spreading their fingers out – onto the fabric.

☞ Draw around the whole hand with a marker.

☞ Cut two pieces of fabric about 2 cm outside the hand outline. Leave a wide wrist opening for the hand to slip into the puppet.

☞ Stitch or sew around the outside of the puppet, leaving the wrist open.

☞ The children can glue on coloured wool, fabric scraps, buttons and other materials to make the features of the puppets.

Stick-figure puppets

You will need:
- popsicle sticks
- felt-tip pens
- paper
- glue

What to do:
- ☞ Grandchildren can paint or draw faces on the sticks.
- ☞ They can cut out a paper shape for a costume and clue this on.

A Short Cut

Cut the fingers off a pair of gloves. Help grandchildren decorate them to make individual finger puppets, for example 'The Three Little Pigs', wolf and wood-cutter.

Finger puppets

You will need:
- paper or material
- felt-tip pens
- wool, odds and ends of material
- glue
- needle and cotton

What to do:
- ☞ Grandchildren place their hand – spreading their fingers out – onto the fabric.
- ☞ Draw around the four fingers with a marker.
- ☞ Cut two pieces of fabric about 2 cm outside the outline of four fingers.
- ☞ Sew or glue around the outside of the finger puppets leaving the opening to slip on the fingers.
- ☞ Grandchildren can draw, or glue on coloured wool, fabric scraps, buttons and other materials to make hair and beards and other features for the puppets.

Box puppets

Box puppets are simple marionette puppets . . .
puppets that work on strings. Grandchildren will love
operating them. Use a clean, empty milk or juice
carton for the head and body and paper strips for
arms and legs.

You will need:
- an empty milk or juice carton
- felt-tip pens
- odds and ends of material to decorate the puppet
- PVA glue
- pencil
- paper
- string

What to do:
- ☛ Help your grandchild make a hole in each side of
  the upper part and lower part of the carton.
- ☛ To make legs and arms, wrap strips of paper tightly
  around a pencil. Fasten the strips. Slide the strips
  off the pencil. You can make two sections for each
  jointed arm and leg.
- ☛ Thread the paper cylinders onto the string to make
  arms and legs.
- ☛ Knot string at the end of each arm and leg.
- ☛ Fasten the string, which will control the arms and
  legs, to two crossed popsicle sticks.
- ☛ The children can decorate the carton making a face
  and clothes.
- ☛ Attach a string to the top part of the carton so the
  'head' can move.
- ☛ The children can practise making the puppets move.
- ☛ If the grandchildren make a few more marionette
  puppets they will be able to put on a performance.

A Moving Hint

The paper bag puppets can be stuffed with newspaper, and a ruler or used lunch-wrap roll can be taped to the bottom. Grandchildren can hold the puppet to make it move.

Paper bag puppets

Paper bag puppets are really simple and easy for very young grandchildren to make and perform with.

You will need:
- paper bags
- PVA glue
- scissors
- felt-tip pens
- scrap paper, wool and other odds and ends.

What to do:
☞ Grandchildren can draw faces on the bags.
☞ Scraps of wool, material and other things can be glued onto the bag.
☞ When the puppets are finished the children can put them over their hands and make their puppet talk.

Performing with puppets

Help grandchildren to make up small stories for their puppets to perform.

Take a part in the play! Tape music – experiment with sound effects. This will add to the performance.

A young grandchild is quite able to be a sound operator and press START when required for a live performance!

A table-top puppet theatre

☛ A large cloth or sheet will hide grandchildren who sit beneath the table. The children can hold the puppets so that they appear at the edge of the table for the performance.

Finger puppet theatres

Use a cereal carton or shoe box to make a theatre for finger puppets.

Paint the box, stand it on end, and cut a window near the top for the puppets so that they can be held up for a performance.

A curtain puppet theatre

Making a portable curtain puppet theatre is a great idea. It can stretch across a doorway and be taken down and stored until needed.

You will need:
- length of material – twice the width of the doorway
- hooks
- stretch wire = width of doorway

What to do:
☛ Stitch a hem across the top of the material in order to thread stretch wire.
☛ Stitch a hem across the bottom of the material.
☛ Attach hooks to either side of doorway.
☛ Estimate height of curtain so it covers grandchildren when they are kneeling.
☛ The curtain can be decorated with fabric paints. Do this outside!

Artworks

If you are an art enthusiast you will not be able to stop yourself joining in art activities with your grandchildren.

If you enjoyed art activities when you were younger or have always wanted to try, now is the time. Join in the creativity and fun with the children.

Who knows? You could even become a second Grandma Moses.

Water-colour Pencils

Good quality water-colour pencils are a very satisfactory art medium for children and grandparents. They are much easier to use than water-colour paints. Artists, young and old, can produce fantastic creative art effects when they use them.

Drawing

Drawing is the most marvellous creative outlet, a wonderful activity for grandchildren of all ages.

Young grandchildren will enjoy experimenting with colour and the texture of the medium they are using. Older grandchildren will enjoy sketching, using only pencils, and a pad.

Grandparents should always have a good supply of drawing pencils (HB or 2B), coloured pencils, felt-tip pens and drawing paper on hand. It pays to invest in a smaller supply of quality pencils, which have strong colours and give the best results.

Keep drawing materials in good condition and in their own special container. Even though drawing fits into the 'non-messy' category, protect table tops and other furniture, especially when using felt-tip pens.

Sketching

A portable sketching kit for older grandchildren can provide the incentive for reluctant drawers. They will need a sketch pad, pencils, an eraser and a sharpener, and a bag to carry them in.

Encourage grandchildren to sketch things they observe around them – inside and outside. As grandchildren become more proficient – expand their range of materials, for example with charcoal pencils.

Collage

Collage – cutting and pasting different materials onto a variety of surfaces – is another activity to keep grandchildren happy for hours. It is a relatively mess-free activity and quick to prepare!

Collect bits and pieces of material suitable for collage in a large box. Separate and store materials such as beads and sequins in one small plastic container, bits of wool and cord in another, etc. Always keep your bits and pieces box filled and up-to-date.

To make a collage

You will need:
- glue or glue sticks
- brushes or popsicle sticks for application
- odds and ends, for example scraps of coloured paper and fabric, wool, old magazines, catalogues and cards, ribbon, wool and string, cotton wool and feathers, pasta, seeds, sticks, leaves etc.
- heavy paper or cardboard, old boxes and containers

What to do:

☛ PVA glue, not paste, works best for collage artwork. It will stick objects heavier than paper. Supervise grandchildren while they are using it! Use a small container of glue and a popsicle stick to apply it. Explain to grandchildren that they need only use a small amount to make things stick.

Grandchildren can:

☛ make 'feely' pictures using materials that feel different;

☛ decorate boxes and other containers;

☛ draw a picture and use different materials to cover it;

☛ make gift cards – big and small.

Painting

Painting is messy . . . but fun!

☛ Most young grandchildren will not draw anything that looks like a known person, animal or object! Up till about four years of age they will be experimenting with colour and their use of pencils, pens and brushes.

☛ At about four years of age they begin to draw or paint symbols. Mostly they draw themselves – and maybe the sun. Then the family and other familiar symbols will come into their artwork.

☛ Don't be surprised if young grandchildren spend only a very short time on one painting. This is quite normal. However, if your grandchild paints one line and then wants a new piece of paper, you can suggest they paint some more on the paper they have.

☛ Avoid showing grandchildren how you draw. Your symbols mightn't look like the real thing to them either! Who said a flying bird has to look like a coat-hanger in the sky?

☛ Don't ask too many probing questions about young grandchildren's artwork, such as 'Where are the legs?' Better to say, 'Tell me about your painting.'

☛ Even if your grandchild was just experimenting with lots of red and big, big brush strokes, he or she will make up a story to keep you happy. Other times there will definitely be a story behind their creative artwork!

Protective clothing

Make sure you and your grandchildren always wear protective clothing. Paint has a way of getting on everything. You can buy commercial plastic protective clothing. An old raincoat, or an old shirt will work just as well. Cut the sleeves back to size to prevent them from dangling in the paint. Keep the clothes to wear at your home!

Brushes

A selection of different-sized brushes are best for young children. Older grandchildren may prefer to use smaller brushes.

To keep brushes soft, grandchildren should clean them when they are finished. Wrap them in plastic wrap for storing.

Encourage children to use a variety of objects to create different effects, for example feathers, sticks, leaves, pieces of sponge, cotton buds, discarded toothbrushes, etc.

Paint

☛ Use a plastic egg carton or an old patty cake tin for an artist's palette.

☛ Give only small quantities of each colour at a time.

☛ You can use yoghurt pots and pack them firmly in a shallow cardboard box. If they are knocked over they will not make too much mess!

Paper

Young grandchildren will find it easier to paint on thick, absorbent paper. You can buy coloured paper at art and craft shops to use for special projects such as birthday cards. Use recycled computer paper or architects' paper. Buy old rolls of wallpaper when they are being sold cheaply.

A Grandparent Handy Hint

Set up the painting activity outdoors whenever possible. Easels, surroundings and grandchildren can be hosed down at the end of painting. This is a great idea for grandparents who are nervy about paint spills on the white floor tiles.

Easels

Easels make painting easier for young grandchildren. You can turn a child's blackboard into an easel by covering it with plastic and using bulldog clips to attach the paper.

Drying and displaying art

Before grandchildren begin painting, make a space to dry wet paintings. They can dry outside or be pegged on a clothes rack inside.

To display paintings you can:

☞ peg them on wire coat-hangers and hang them from hooks on the wall or ceiling;

☞ hang them on skirt-hangers on a hook on the wall. Different paintings can be displayed on top.

Water painting

This is a brilliant painting activity for young grandchildren, perfect for a hot day.

You will need:

- an assortment of paint brushes – pastry brushes to real paint brushes
- small bucket of water

What to do:
Encourage grandchildren to paint fences, paths, walls, trees and anything else they choose.

Finger painting

Finger painting is about the messiest of painting but lots of fun.

Use plastic sheeting as a tablecloth. Prepare finger paint the night before or in time for the paint to cool.

Be prepared to gather up grandchild at the conclusion of painting and deposit in a cleaning area to wash. A bucket of water and cloth nearby is another alternative.

Have string and pegs ready for hanging paintings.

Finger paint recipes

Recipe 1

Ingredients:
- 1 cup of cornflour
- a little cold water
- 3 cups of boiling water
- Food colouring or poster paint

What to do:
- ☞ Mix the cornflour with a little cold water to make a smooth paste.
- ☞ Slowly pour on boiling water, stirring all the time until the mixture thickens.
- ☞ Add enough colouring to make a strong colour.
- ☞ Leave the finger paint to cool.

Recipe 2

Add dry powder paint to mixed wallpaper paste.

Doing finger painting

What you need:

- finger paint (limit colours for young grandchildren – blue and yellow are good to begin with and young grandchildren will discover that when blue and yellow are mixed together you get green!)
- large sheets of paper with a smooth slippery surface
- tin tray, or use of a table top protected with large sheets of plastic

What to do:

☞ Spread large dollops of colour thinly with your fingers in a large tin tray or on a plastic sheet on the table.

☞ Make a pattern or drawing in paint using fingers.

☞ Lay a sheet of paper over the pattern or drawing.

☞ Peel paper off gently and hang up to dry.

Painting techniques

There are numerous different painting techniques which can keep grandchildren challenged. Once they have mastered a few techniques, encourage older grandchildren to combine them in one piece of artwork. For instance, splatter painting can be used as a background or for adding detail to a broadly finished artwork.

Paint-blowing

Paint-blowing is best for older grandchildren. Young grandchildren will tend to suck not blow!

You will need:
- paint – 2 or 3 colours
- straws, funnel or cotton reel
- paper

What to do:
☛ Place a dribble of thin paint on the paper.
☛ Let grandchildren blow the paint around the surface of the paper through a funnel, straw or cotton reel to create fantastic patterns.
☛ Paint-blowing over large sheets of paper makes great wrapping paper.

Dot paintings

Older grandchildren can use the technique of tiny dots of colour to create a drawing or painting. This activity is relaxing for grandparents. It can take a long time to complete a dot painting!

You will need:
- drawing paper (for example recycled computer paper, etc.)
- paints, coloured pencils, or fine pointed felt-tip pens
- a fine brush

What to do:
☛ Grandchildren can lightly sketch their picture in pencil before beginning the technique.
☛ Visit the library and find some art books to show how Impressionist artists such as Monet and Seurat used this technique.

Splatter painting

Splatter painting is another interesting technique which grandchildren may like to try. Splattered artwork makes stunning wrapping paper. This is an activity which is ideal for outdoors!

You will need:
- containers of paint
- a brush – old toothbrushes are ideal – for each container
- paper

What to do:
- ☛ Spread paper on a flat surface – preferably grass!
- ☛ Show grandchildren how to dip the brush in paint and flick the brush with their fingers so the paint flies onto the paper.
- ☛ A toothbrush and small piece of fine wire will also create an interesting splatter effect on paper.

Printing

Printing is a second cousin of painting . . . very messy, but great fun! Grandchildren can add details to fingerprints to change them into little people, insects, flowers or anything they can think of. Pets paw prints are also effective! A container of water to wash hands and feet after the activity is essential.

Potato prints

You will need:
- potatoes
- thick paint – two or three different colours
- trays lined with sponge – one for each colour

What to do:
- ☛ Pour paint into each tray.
- ☛ Cut potatoes in half. They can be used to make different patterns.
- ☛ You can also cut shapes into each half by carving away the parts of the potato you don't want. Stars, triangles and squares make interesting print patterns.
- ☛ Press potatoes into sponge then print firmly on paper.
- ☛ Grandchildren can make patterns or pictures. They can also experiment by using different fruit and vegetables such as carrots, broccoli, lemons and celery, as well as other objects.

Fingerprints, handprints and footprints

This is definitely an outdoor activity! Handprints and footprints of grandchildren can make very sentimental mementoes to keep!

You will need:
- thick paint – two or three different colours
- trays lined with sponge – one for each colour (for footprinting they will need to be big enough to fit feet!)
- large sheets of paper

What to do:
- ☛ Pour paint into each tray.
- ☛ Grandchildren press fingers, hands or feet into sponge, then print firmly on paper.
- ☛ Prints can be used to make pictures or patterns.

Body shapes

Grandchildren will see their actual size and shape when they do this activity.

You will need:
- a sheet of paper as big as your grandchild
- thick pencil or crayon
- paint and brushes

What to do:
- ☛ Place paper on a smooth hard floor.
- ☛ Ask grandchild to lie on paper. Make sure fingers are spread out so the pencil mark can go around each one.
- ☛ Draw around the grandchild with a thick pencil or crayon.
- ☛ Grandchildren can draw or paint their hair, face and clothes on their body shape afterwards.
- ☛ Cut out shape to pin on wall.
- ☛ You can keep your grandchild's body shape at your home. Compare from time to time to see how the child has grown. Or they can take their body shape home with them!
- ☛ For fun . . . swap roles. You lie on the floor and ask grandchildren to draw around you. (Don't wear your best Armani suit!)

Craft
works

Make sure grandchildren ride their hobby horse in a safe place. Watch ornaments, TV, furniture, etc. if hobby horse is galloped indoors.

Making a hobby horse

A hobby horse is a fun thing for grandchildren to make. Keep the hobby horse stabled at your place for play.

To make the horse

What you need:
- a large paper bag
- a broom or mop
- felt pens
- newspaper for stuffing
- extra paper to make a mane and ears
- lengths of cord or masking tape

What to do:
- ☛ Draw a face on the paper bag.
- ☛ Stick on ears.
- ☛ Cut paper into strips and stick on to make a mane.
- ☛ Put the head over the broom or mop.
- ☛ Stuff it with extra paper to make a head shape.
- ☛ Fasten the head on firmly with cord or masking tape.
- ☛ Make some reins.

Sammy Snake

To make a snake

You will need:
- a colourful odd sock
- old newspaper
- coloured paper, stickers, buttons and odds and ends
- PVA glue
- needle and thread

What to do:
- ☞ Grandchildren tear newspaper into small pieces for the filling. (This is a great fine-motor activity as well as one that takes a long time!)
- ☞ They can fill their snake when they have torn enough paper – making sure to push it right down to the toe.
- ☞ Sew or glue end of sock.
- ☞ Stickers or buttons can be used for the face. Paper stripes and spots can be glued onto the body.

Snake draught stopper

Save odd socks. Older grandchildren can use them to make a useful 'draught stopper'. It makes a great gift – or a really, really, really long toy snake for a younger brother or sister.

You will need:
- about ten old and/or odd socks (bright socks look better)
- old stockings or material for stuffing
- coloured wool
- darning needle
- buttons for eyes, ribbon for neck tie

What to do:
- ☞ Cut toe ends off all but one of the socks.
- ☞ Stuff the one toe end firmly, then sew on a sock leg with a darning needle and coloured wool.
- ☞ Now stuff this sock leg, then sew on another sock leg, and stuff it and so on until you come to the end.
- ☞ Sew buttons on for eyes and tie the ribbon around the neck.
- ☞ Bingo! An environmentally friendly snake draft stopper!

Handy hint

Commercial wallpaper pastes work well too.

Use small containers of paste and refill them. There is not so much wastage or mess if they are tipped over!

Papier mâché

Papier mâché is a great medium for grandchildren. Applying layer after layer of soggy paper is slow but a very calming and soothing activity.

Papier mâché can be used to make useful gifts, puppet heads, masks, piggy bank money-boxes and other things.

You can buy papier mâché mixture from craft shops or use paper and paste.

Papier mâché paste recipe

Ingredients:
- 6 tablespoons cornflour
- 2 cups boiling water
- 1/2 cup cold water

What to do:
- ☛ Blend 6 tablespoons cornflour with 1/2 cup of cold water.
- ☛ Add 2 cups of boiling water and boil for one minute until it becomes clear. (If it is too thick, add a little more water.)

A papier mâché dish

You will need:
- non-toxic paste or wallpaper paste
- petroleum jelly
- used paper torn into strips about 2 cm by 15 cm
- a plate or bowl to use as a mould
- acrylic paint

What to do:
- ☛ Grease the mould well with petroleum jelly so papier mâché will lift off when it is completed.
- ☛ Cover used paper strips lavishly with paste.
- ☛ Apply layer after layer to the mould - a few layers each day until the desired thickness is reached.
- ☛ Make the last few layers from white paper.
- ☛ When it is dry, paint the inside and outside of the dish with a background colour.
- ☛ When this is dry grandchildren can add their own decorative designs.

Papier mâché masks

This is definitely a project for when older grandchildren are staying for a few days.

You will need:
- non-toxic wallpaper paste
- 1 balloon
- used paper torn into strips about 2 cm by 15 cm

What to do:
- ☛ Blow up balloon.
- ☛ Cover newspaper strips lavishly with paste.
- ☛ Apply two or three layers to the balloon at a time. Allow to dry quickly outside to prevent mildew.
- ☛ When the papier mâché is strong enough burst the balloon inside with a pin.
- ☛ Cut the papier mâché shape in half. You will have two shapes for masks.
- ☛ Decorate them and add ties to fasten.

Making musical instruments

Musical instruments can be very easy and cheap to make.

Making music with grandchildren will provide hours of entertainment and fun.

Why not make a comb synthesiser? Grandparents will remember playing these musical instruments when they were young. Why not make a few and form a comb band? All you need to do is wrap a few layers of tissue paper around a comb. Hold it to your lips and hum! Can your grandchildren recognise the tune?

Easy instruments to make

☛ Trumpets and bugles can be made from cardboard tubes.

☛ Drums can be made from plastic containers, buckets and mixing bowls turned upside down. Different skins such as plastic, thin rubber sheet or wrapping paper can be stretched across them to make different sounds. Fasten the skins with cord or elastic.

☛ Cymbals from pot lids . . . if you really feel they will add to a grandchild's musical development at your home and you don't mind the noise!

☛ Musical chimes from different bottles or jars containing different levels of water. Tap gently with spoons!

☛ Rhythm sticks from short lengths of dowel or an old broomstick, sawn off and sanded at the ends. Grandchildren can tap out the rhythm of songs they know.

☛ Shakers or castanets can be made by filling two paper cups or plastic containers with uncooked rice, dried pasta, or split peas. Join the containers together with tape. Grandchildren can shake out rhythms with them.

☛ Bells threaded onto elastic make lovely, 'gentle' jingly music.

Sanity Advice

Plastic containers make much quieter drums than tins, pots and pans!

Environmental activities

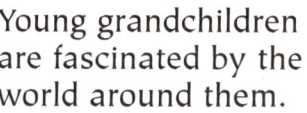

Young grandchildren are fascinated by the world around them.

Enjoying nature with young grandchildren can be as simple as taking a walk in the rain and counting the earthworms that have escaped from their flooded burrows.

Being outdoors develops an awareness of the environment. Older grandchildren will see positive ways to sustain their environment when they take part in environmental activities.

Bark and leaf rubbings

Grandchildren will discover the texture of leaves and bark on trees when they make bark and leaf rubbings. Older grandchildren can use their rubbings to make gift cards or in collages.

To make a rubbing

You will need:
- a collection of leaves and/or access to trees
- paper
- tape
- crayons or pastels

What to do:
- ☞ Tape the paper to a tree.
- ☞ Rub an unwrapped crayon or pastel, using even strokes over the paper.
- ☞ To make a leaf rubbing, place a sheet of paper over a leaf with the veins facing up.

Pressing garden flowers

Many grandparents will remember collecting and pressing flowers to make cards and pictures when they were children.

Once grandchildren have a collection of dried pressed flowers they can use them to create attractive cards and artwork.

Pressed flowers

You will need:
- small flowers and leaves from the garden (Experiment with different flowers. Flowers such as daisies and violets work well.)
- old telephone book
- sheets of kitchen paper towel
- heavy weight such as a brick

What to do:
- ☛ Place the flowers and leaves between two pieces of kitchen paper towel. Lie them flat so all petals are seen.
- ☛ Put them at twenty-page intervals in the old telephone book.
- ☛ Weight the telephone book with heavy books or a brick.
- ☛ It takes several weeks for the flowers to dry and be ready to be used on further artwork.

Care for the Environment!

Leave wildflowers where you find them.

Dried flower cards

You will need:
- a collection of dried pressed small flowers and leaves.
- card
- coloured pencils or textas
- glue

What to do:
- ☛ Fold card.
- ☛ Place dried flowers in a design on the front. Leaves, bits of ribbon, etc. can be added, too.
- ☛ When grandchildren are happy with their arrangement they can glue their design down.
- ☛ Help young grandchildren with writing to complete their card.

Bird-feeding tray

When grandchildren make a bird-feeding tray you will be able to attract birds to your garden. Fill it with seeds or other suitable food for the birds that visit your area. Sit quietly with grandchildren and watch the birds come to your feeding tray.

Making the tray

You will need:
- a foil tray or tin tray
- string

What to do:

☛ Make nail holes in the tin or foil tray.

☛ Knot a long string through each hole.

☛ Hang the tray from a branch of a tree. Choose a safe place that cats can't reach.

A mini worm farm

Earthworms do not make the Top Ten Most Popular Creature List but they are very important for our environment. Making a wormery will help grandchildren understand the importance of worms for the soil. (Worms turn over the soil just like a farmer with a hoe, and let in essential air and water.)

Making the wormery

You will need:
- a large glass jar
- soil
- sand
- vegetable scraps or compost
- black plastic or paper
- three or four worms
- panty hose
- rubber bands

What to do:
- ☛ Fill the jar 3/4 full with layers of soil and sand.
- ☛ Cover with vegetable scraps or compost.
- ☛ Place three or four worms in container.
- ☛ Cover with panty hose and fasten with rubber bands.
- ☛ Tape some black plastic or paper around the jar to keep out the light. (Worms don't like the light.)
- ☛ Place the jar in a cool spot.

An on-going activity

A worm farm is on-going. Food scraps need to be added every week. Contents of the jar need to be sprinkled with water so they are moist, but not soggy wet.
- ☛ Make sure grandchildren return the worms to the soil when they have finished observing them.
- ☛ Larger, outdoor worm farms can be successfully developed in plastic foam fruit boxes stacked on top of each other, or you can buy a commercial worm farm.

Collecting worms

You can collect worms without digging up your garden if you leave some old carpet or black plastic on a section of mulch or lawn overnight.

Check underneath in the morning.

Worm watching

Grandchildren can watch and record the movement of the worms. If the black paper sleeve covers the container for most of the time, the worms will feed up against the inside walls.

At the end of your worm watching, you can count the number of worms if you tip out the contents of your wormery and use a garden sieve.

Have grandchildren noticed any changes inside the jar?

☛ Are there any worm castings?
☛ What has happened to the layers of sand and soil?
☛ Are there any visible tunnels?
☛ What else can they see?

A mini compost bin

When you make a mini compost bin it will help grandchildren to understand the value of reusing resources.

Making the 'bin'

You will need:

- a large clear plastic juice bottle
- 2 cups of finely chopped fruit or vegetable scraps
- 1 cup of crushed dry leaves
- 1 cup of torn newspaper
- 2 cups of garden soil
- grass clippings
- spoon
- 1 dessertspoon of organic fertiliser
- adhesive tape

What to do:

☞ Cut the top from the large plastic bottle.

☞ Fill the bottle starting with a layer of soil, then fruit or vegetable scraps.

☞ Cover with soil and sprinkle some fertiliser over it.

☞ Continue to build up layers using leaves, grass and newspaper.

☞ Finish with a layer of soil and fertiliser.

☞ Spray the surface with water.

☞ Tape the top of the bottle back on.

Natural Fertiliser

Compost is crumbly material produced from decaying vegetable and garden waste. It can be used as a plant fertiliser or soil conditioner.

Compost:

- ☞ saves money (we have to pay people to take away our waste);
- ☞ reduces the demand for landfill sites;
- ☞ produces great fertiliser.

An on-going activity

Grandchildren can observe their mini compost bin for three or four weeks. They can look for changes in layers, colour, size and shape of the plant material. Is there any mould growing? Are there any small creatures feeding on the plant material?

Wind chimes

Help grandchildren to make simple wind chimes. Hang them in the garden or inside the house where a breeze can move them. The tinkling sounds will add delight to a windy day.

To make your chimes

You will need:
- a variety of materials such as small clay shapes, bamboo, shells, seed pods, small metal nuts, etc.
- fishing line
- a small tree branch or piece of wood
- drill

What to do:
- ☞ Test and decide which materials will make the best sound.
- ☞ Drill holes in materials and help grandchildren to tie the materials to the branch.
- ☞ Hang them where you can enjoy their music.

Make a hairy grass caterpillar

Grandchildren will be aware of the development of plants as they watch their caterpillar become hairy!

They can take their newly planted caterpillar home to care for it or watch its development when they visit your home.

Making the caterpillar

You will need:

- a length of 20 cm stocking or leg of a pair of panty hose which includes the foot
- lentils, coloured paper scraps or buttons for eyes, nose and mouth
- 1 elastic band
- 1 handful of grass seed
- 2 handfuls of potting mix
- water
- a shallow dish
- rubber gloves
- glue

What to do:

☞ Wearing rubber gloves mix the grass seed with the potting mix.

☞ Fill the stocking with the mixture, making it look like a sausage.

☞ Fasten the end with the elastic band.

☞ Glue a face onto the caterpillar.

☞ Pour water into the dish and place the caterpillar in it.

☞ Place the dish near sunlight so the grass will grow.

☞ Replace water frequently to prevent it becoming smelly.

☞ The caterpillar will become hairy in several weeks time.

☞ Grandchildren can give the caterpillar a haircut and watch the grass grow again.

Part 3:

Games to play

Child play
and games

Ordinary, everyday,
unstructured play
gives grandchildren
the opportunity to
extend their creativity
and imagination.

Join in with your grandchildren. Enter their wonderful, private world of play. Become a shopkeeper, an aeroplane, a friendly dinosaur, a flesh-eating monster.

Young grandchildren need only a few simple toys or an idea from you to spark off imaginative play.

Remember, the best fun comes from informal and spontaneous games.

However, having some equipment and ideas for structured games on hand is a great survival strategy for grandparents.

There are two main groups of games: 'quiet' games and 'energetic' games. Grandparents need to have a repertoire of both to survive well.

'Quiet' games

'Quiet' games, such as board games and cards, have been old favourites for years. You will find they still fascinate grandchildren and keep them 'reasonably' quiet and happy for some time.

A Grandparent Golden Hint

Stop playing if you find yourself getting irritated or cross.

A 'No Talking' Challenge

'Energetic' games can become 'quiet' games by adding the challenge of a 'No Talking' rule.

Handy hints for 'quiet' games

☞ Explain the structure and rules of the game carefully to the children.
☞ Simplify or change the rules for younger grandchildren in order to keep them in the play.
☞ Vary games. Don't get stuck on family favourites.
☞ Keep the action moving . . . this prevents squabbles!
☞ Finish the game while the interest is high.

Grandparents' rules for 'quiet' games

☞ Fair play at all times.
☞ Everyone must agree on the rules for each game and follow them.
☞ Accept decisions of the umpire and/or officials . . . (usually a grandparent!) as final!

Scoring

If interest in a game begins to fall, play for a score. Scoring should be used to encourage each player to play better . . . not to prove that one player is better than another.

When scoring becomes more important than playing, abandon the game. Then start again making it a co-operative rather than a competitive event.

Number of players

The number of players taking part can affect a game enormously.

A game of chasey with a grandparent and grandchild is quite different from playing chasey with the family.

If a game with the family gets too chaotic, divide into smaller groups or several teams.

If a game is too dull, up the challenge by selecting more than one person to be 'it'.

Where to play?

Be ready to alter rules because of the size of a room or area, and its obstacles, such as furniture or large trees!

Time

Limit the time of a game to create challenges and excitement as players try to beat the clock.

Extend the time if young grandchildren are becoming frustrated and upset.

Co-operation, socialisation and collaboration

A game works when players are co-operating, socialising and collaborating. Grandchildren can learn life skills when, as players, they concentrate, solve problems and keep their part of the game working.

Electronic games

Electronic games are 'cool' entertainment that grandchildren revel in. They are interactive and competitive. Many involve shooting computerised people-like icons or escaping from amazing perils and dangers – the player represented by an icon.

Beware! Electronic games are addictive – no matter what your age!

Visit an electronic game shop with your grandchildren or hire games from commercial outlets to be in on this 'cool' entertainment.

You and your grandchildren will learn good hand-eye co-ordination skills. However, when grandchildren are with you, balance the variety of games played. Be as active as possible.

Too long in front of a computer, too much sedentary work or recreation, is not good for grandchildren or grandparents' muscles and joints!

Board games

Traditional board games are still brilliant entertainment for grandchildren. Games such as Snakes and Ladders, Ludo, Monopoly, Cluedo and Scrabble will all prove popular.

If you are a chess enthusiast, or wish you had learnt chess, borrow or buy a 'How to play Chess' book. Now is the time to learn with grandchildren.

Handy hints

☛ Keep board games in a safe place.
☛ Make sure you pack the game accessories carefully. (It's infuriating if you are missing a Q or Z from Scrabble!)

Putting on a play

Children love to act, to take part in a performance. Grandchildren, friends and family can put on a play.

If there is a scarcity of actors, a grandparent and a single grandchild can cope quite well by taking on multiple roles.

A Grandparent Golden Hint

The key to a successful performance is lots and lots of rehearsals!

Rehearsals will take up lots and lots of time. Relax and supervise or just relax!

Guidelines for putting on a play

☛ It is best to start with a story everybody knows. Extra bits can be added or taken out of the plot where necessary. The best plays are those that are created by grandchildren themselves.

☛ Decide on who is going to play which parts. An older grandchild or grandparent taking the part of narrator will keep the action moving.

☛ Any fights should be in slow motion and obviously fake. Characters should not touch each other!

☛ Imaginary movements should be done the same way by all characters, for instance shutting a door in or out!

☛ Encourage grandchildren to speak up and sing out. Dancing and movements should be clear and take part at the front of the stage.

☛ Make-up, lights, music, and of course a curtain of some kind, will add to the thrill of performing.

☛ Costumes can be as simple as ears, painted whiskers and a tail to indicate a character.

☛ A space for the actors to perform and one for the audience is an absolute necessity.

Playing cards

A pack of 52 playing cards is fantastic basic equipment for amusing grandchildren. It is a great way for your family, young and old, to have fun and play together.

There are an enormous number of card games. Familiarise young grandchildren with the organisation of a pack of cards. Play simple card games first and advance to the more complicated ones.

Making card houses and buildings is also a great way to while away a rainy day. How big can you make your card house? How tall can you make your card building? No blowing! No heavy breathing!

Concentration

Players must concentrate and remember where cards are placed in order to match pairs.

You will need: One deck of cards

Number of players: Two or more

How to play:
- ☞ Dealer places all cards face down on the table.
- ☞ Each player can turn over two cards. If they match they keep the pair. If not the cards are placed face down again in their place, and it is the next player's turn.
- ☞ The person with the most pairs at the end of the game wins.

Pick up

You will need: One pack of cards

Number of players: Two, three or four

How to play:
- ☞ Choose a player to shuffle and deal the card pack.
- ☞ The dealer will lay cards out in random fashion, face down.
- ☞ Each player selects a suit (hearts, diamonds, clubs or spades) which is different from the other players.
- ☞ Players take turns picking up one card at a time. (Do not let other players see the card!) If the card is from the suit they have selected, the player keeps it and places it in front of them. If not they replace it in the same position – face down.
- ☞ The first player to collect five cards from their selected suit is the winner.

Fish

This is a simple card game where players 'fish' for cards to make pairs. For older players, they can 'fish' to make four of a kind.

You will need: One deck of cards

Number of players. Two and more

How to play:
- ☞ Each player is dealt five cards. The remaining cards are placed in the centre of the table.
- ☞ The aim of the game is to make two of a kind.
- ☞ It begins when the player on the left of the dealer asks, 'Can I have a king?'
- ☞ The player asked has to agree to this request unless they don't have that card. If this is the case they answer, 'Fish!'
- ☞ The first player has then to pick up a card from the centre stack and the next player takes his turn.
- ☞ When a player gets two of a kind, he or she shows them and puts them face up.
- ☞ This also ends that player's turn.
- ☞ The winner is the first player to get rid of their cards or the player with the most pairs when there aren't any cards left to pick up from the centre.

Pairs

You will need: A pack of cards

Number of players: Two or more

How to play:
- ☞ Remove the aces, tens, jacks, queens and kings.
- ☞ Shuffle the rest of the pack.
- ☞ Lay out eight cards in a row, face up.
- ☞ Cover these with another eight cards face up.
- ☞ Repeat until you have four cards in each of the eight stacks.
- ☞ Players take turns to pick up pairs of like cards such as two fours, two nines, any two that match.
- ☞ If three like numbers appear,they only pick up two.
- ☞ The winner is the player who pairs all the cards.

Animal noises

A noisy and tricky game in which players have to concentrate as well as make animal noises. The umpire should be on hand to give decisions!

You will need: A pack of cards

Number of players: Four – six

How to play:
- ☞ A player deals the pack out equally to all players, face down.
- ☞ Players choose to be an animal that has a distinctive sound, for example cat, lion, dog, parrot.
- ☞ Players turn over their top cards in turn.
- ☞ When a card is turned over that matches one already turned over, the first of the two players to call out the animal sound of his opponent wins the other's stack. For instance, if the lion turns over a king and the cat has a king on the top of his face-up stack, the 'lion' will try to 'meow' while the cat will try to 'roar'.

Sevens

An old favourite, which sets grandchildren on the road to playing more complicated card games.

You will need: One pack of cards with the Jokers removed

Number of players: Two or more

How to play:
- ☛ The aim is to be the first player to run out of cards.
- ☛ Shuffle the cards and decide who will deal.
- ☛ The dealer deals seven cards to each player.
- ☛ The remaining cards are placed face down in a pack in the centre.
- ☛ Players check for a seven in their hand.
- ☛ The player on the right of the dealer starts.
- ☛ They can put down any seven in their hand plus any other cards of the same suit (six, five, etc.) so long as the cards run in numerical order, up or down from seven.
- ☛ If the player doesn't have a seven in their hand they pick up the top card from the pack. If a seven is picked up they may place it down, along with cards of the same suit if they have them.
- ☛ The player's turn is over if they have put down all the cards they can.
- ☛ The next player can add to an existing run or begin a new run with a seven.
- ☛ If a player runs out of cards, they can pick up the top card from the pack and start again.
- ☛ The winner is the first player to run out of cards by placing them correctly.

'Energetic' games

Play 'energetic' games
that involve a variety
of movements . . .
hopping, skipping,
running, jumping,
balancing, throwing
and catching. They
are fun and will
develop
grandchildren's eye-
hand co-ordination
and other physical
skills. They are also
excellent for using up
buckets of
grandchildren's
energy!

Materials

A change of materials can alter an energetic game completely.

Try playing a bat and ball game with a cardboard tube and a balloon!

The size of balls used will also change the level of difficulty of certain games. (See rules for 'Quiet' games.)

Using playground equipment

When you take young grandchildren to parks, playing on playground equipment . . . climbing ladders, swinging on bars, balancing on tyres and sliding down poles . . . is not only fun but improves grandchildren's strength and co-ordination, and uses lots of energy!

Rope games

A length of rope is useful for playing many games.

Jump rope

You will need:
- a length of rope
- bean bag, or half a sock filled with dried beans.

How to play:
- Tie the bean bag to the end of the rope.
- Swing the rope around just above the ground.
- Grandchildren jump over the rope as it comes around.

Rules:
- When the rope hits someone they are out.
- The winner is the last one in. (Make sure all players take a turn at swinging the rope around!)

Skipping

Skipping is fun and develops co-ordination for grandchildren. It works well with rhythm chants and rhymes. Can you remember some of the chants you used for skipping?

Skipping with one 'ender'

Skipping with one rope which is turned by 'enders' is the easiest to learn. Young grandchildren only have to learn to jump. A grandparent can turn one end of the the rope, the other can be tied to a fence or tree.

An Easy Bean Bag

An easy bean bag can be made by using old socks. Fill one old sock with dried beans. Tuck the sock inside a mate so the beans won't fall out. Stitching or gluing will make it secure.

Bean bag games

Bean bags are a great substitute for balls – especially for young grandchildren. They are safe for throwing and catching games, and are easy to grasp.

If you have a 'cleared' space inside your house bean bags are great to use on a rainy day.

Bean bags are fabric bags made by sewing two pieces of fabric (15 cm x 15 cm) together.

They can be filled with dried beans, peas or rice.

A bean bag obstacle course

A bean bag obstacle course is challenging and fun! Grandchildren can help mark the obstacle course in the garden.

If you have a safe, cleared space in your house and feel comfortable with this, grandchildren could play this inside on a rainy day!!

Ideas for the obstacle course

☞ Jump over a broom, or beach towel.
☞ Walk along a curvy rope.
☞ Run around a chair or tree.
☞ Crawl through a large box or tyre.
☞ Thread your body through a hoop, or large box.
☞ Jump or step over a series of staggered tyres on the ground.
☞ Crawl through a chair.
☞ Hop over the rungs of a ladder on the ground.

What you could use:

☞ ladder
☞ rope
☞ chair
☞ hoops

☞ broom
☞ cardboard boxes
☞ beach towel

You will need:

☞ a bean bag
☞ objects to make a simple obstacle course such as large cardboard boxes, hessian bags, ropes, a tyre or a hoop

How to play:

☞ Grandchildren balance the bean bag on parts of their body without touching it with their hands while going through the obstacle course from start to finish.
☞ For their next turn they must think of another way to balance the bean bag: on their head, under their arm, under their chin, jump with it between their knees, between their elbows and their wrists. Grandparents will just have to join in this fun!

Ball games

Throwing, catching, kicking, bouncing and dribbling balls are all skills that grandchildren will develop when they play ball games.

Use a variety of soft, medium-sized balls, balloons and light beach balls.

Playing simple mini versions of sports will help grandchildren's co-ordination and movement techniques. It will also help your grandchildren develop sportsmanship and team spirit . . . as long as grandparents don't show superior skills and win every time!

Handy ball rules

☛ Large balls are best for a small grandchild to use. (A 15–20 cm diameter ball of foam or soft vinyl is a good size for the early years.)
☛ Small balls are for a bigger grandchild.

Balloons are also friendly to use to help develop throwing and catching skills.

Catching and throwing skills

☛ You can help very young grandchildren to catch a ball successfully if they cup their hands together in front.
☛ Prompt them to 'catch' the ball. Then prompt them to throw the ball back to you.
☛ In the beginning stand very close to the child. Move further away as grandchildren learn to successfully catch the ball.
☛ Give lots of cheering and encouragement.

A basketball ring in your garden will be enjoyed by older grandchildren who can use it to improve their goal-shooting.

Ball tricks

Many grandparents will remember ball games and tricks they played as children. Ball tricks all work to make good ball handlers.

Grandchildren can bounce the ball on the ground and then repeat the tricks by bouncing the ball against a wall.

How many times can grandchildren do them?

Do they improve as they keep practising?

Try:

- ☛ Bouncing the ball five times with the right hand, catch it and then five times with the left hand.
- ☛ Throw the ball up in the air and clap hands before catching it.
- ☛ Throw the ball up in the air and clap hands behind the back.
- ☛ Throw the ball from the right hand to the left hand and then vice versa.
- ☛ Bounce the ball on the ground, turn around and catch it.

Bat and ball games

If you have an old broomstick lying around, and you're a 'handy' grandparent, you can make a bat and ball game that will keep grandchildren occupied for hours. It also stops balls vanishing over neighbours' fences!

Keeping the ball in the garden

You will need:
- 1 broomstick
- drill
- knife
- tennis ball
- rope
- table tennis bats

What to do:
- Sharpen one end of the broomstick.
- Drill a hole five centimetres from the top of the other end.
- Drill a hole right through a tennis ball.
- Thread rope through the tennis ball. Tie a knot at the end so the ball will not slip off.
- Tie the other end of the rope through the hole in the broomstick, knotting it so it doesn't slip through.
- Hammer broomstick into the ground.
- Players stand opposite each other and take turns to hit the ball with bats.

Frisbees

Frisbees are fun to throw to each other.
- Choose a park or another open space.
- The frisbee (or a plastic plate) needs to be held horizontally and tossed to launch into the air.

Quoits

Quoits is a traditional game which is great fun and tests throwing skills. Hunt out your old set of quoits or make one.

Home-made quoits set

You will need:
- ☞ empty plastic drink bottle
- ☞ stones
- ☞ metal coat-hangers

What to do:
- ☞ Place stones in an empty drink bottle to stop it falling over and fasten the lid on again.
- ☞ To make hoops, untwist the handle section of a coat-hanger and re-twist the wire to make circles. Or cut off the handles with wire cutters and use the remainder to make circles.

A more temporary alternative is to cut out the centre of paper plates and place a stick in the ground.

The stick must stand up straight about 20 cm from the ground.

How to play:
- ☞ For the first alternative, place bottle on ground.
- ☞ Mark a spot for each grandchild to throw from. (Older grandchildren can have a handicap!)
- ☞ Each player has 10 throws at a time.
- ☞ Keep score.
- ☞ The person who hoops the most quoits over the bottle is a winner.

The idea of the game using the temporary quoits set is to take turns and toss the 'rings' over the stick.

Party games

Party games are
absolutely essential to
a successful party.
Add games you played
as a child to your list.

Party game hints

☛ Make a list of games ahead of time.

☛ Have a balance of 'quiet' and 'energetic' games.

☛ Select more games than you think you'll need.

☛ Include several indoor games in case of bad weather.

☛ Explain each game to the children.

☛ Make a run-through a rehearsal!

☛ Keep the games moving.

☛ Repeat a game if it went well.

☛ Have equipment handy, so there's no break in program while you search for pens and pencils.

☛ If the game carries a prize or prizes say so beforehand.

☛ Control the games. Be fair. See that each child gets a chance to enjoy the games. Vary team leaders. Ignore grumblers.

Never force a child to join in. Let them stand by you. Chances are they will join in next time.

Chinese whispers

Players sit in a line or circle. Tell one of them a funny sentence.

This player must whisper the message to the next, who must whisper what they think they heard to the next player and on it goes down the line.

The last player must tell everyone the message. (It is amazing how the original message will be changed.)

Rule: No repeating the message. Players are given only one chance to hear it.

Marshmallow relay

What you will need:
- toothpicks
- marshmallows
- two bowls

Players: Two teams

How to play:
- Two teams sit on the ground in line.
- Each child has a toothpick.
- Each leader has a small dish containing marshmallows – one for each team member.
- On signal, each leader offers a marshmallow to the team member sitting behind him. Each team member must eat a marshmallow using their toothpick. The team leader is last to finish.
- The team that finishes first is the winner.

Balloon hop relay

You will need: Balloons

Players: Minimum number of children – Six

How to play:
- A balloon is held behind one knee while hopping on the other leg.
- Each player must reach a predetermined point, with their balloon held safely behind their knee. (This needs quite a bit of balance. No hands are allowed to touch the balloon!)
- Each player leaves their balloon and returns to their place in their team.
- The next player in the team takes a turn.
- The team who finishes first is the winner.

The chocolate game

Players: Six or more

You will need:
- a large block of chocolate (one marked out in squares)
- a knife, fork and spoon
- a dice

How to play:
- Chocolate, knife, fork and spoon are placed on a table nearby.
- Children sit in a circle or in two teams.
- The first player to throw a six, hops up to the table and cuts a square of chocolate. They must use the knife, fork and spoon to eat the chocolate without touching it!
- If someone else throws a six they lose their turn at eating the chocolate.

Rule: Set a number of pieces that one player may eat before someone throws a six, for example five!

Variations: If players have to put on gloves, scarf and hat before they can eat the chocolate it adds to the fun.

The memory game

What you need:
- ☛ a tray containing a variety of objects such as a button, pen, pencil, hair clip, toy car, spoon, stamp, apple, etc.
- ☛ pencils and paper for each player

Number of players: Four or more

How to play:
- ☛ Leave the tray on view for a few minutes.
- ☛ Cover the tray.
- ☛ Players list the objects they remember.
- ☛ At the end of the time limit the winner is the player with the most correct objects on their list.

Variations:
- ☛ Vary the number of objects according to children's ages, from ten for seven-year-olds to about twenty for ten-year-olds.
- ☛ Remove one or two objects at a time. Ask players to write down the objects removed.